MULTI-TURRETED TANKS

Books LLC®, Wiki Series, Memphis, USA, 2011. ISBN: 9781155227979. www.booksllc.net
Copyright: http://creativecommons.org/licenses/by-sa/3.0/deed.en

Table of Contents

Char 2C 1	SMK tank 9	T-35 20
Cruiser Mk I 4	T-100 tank 9	Type 95 Heavy Tank 22
FCM F1 5	T-24 tank 9	Vickers 6-Ton 22
Medium Mark III 7	T-26 10	Vickers A1E1 Independent 24
Neubaufahrzeug 8	T-28 19	

Introduction

Purchase of this book entitles you to a free trial membership in the publisher's book club at www.booksllc.net. (Time limited offer.) Simply enter the barcode number from the back cover onto the membership form. The book club entitles you to select from hundreds of thousands of books at no additional charge. You can also download a digital copy of this and related books to read on the go. Simply enter the title or subject onto the search form to find them.

Each chapter in this book ends with a URL to a hyperlinked online version. Type the URL exactly as it appears. If you change the URL's capitalization it won't work. Use the online version to access related pages, websites, footnotes, tables, color photos, updates. Click the version history tab to see the chapter's contributors. Click the edit link to suggest changes.

A large and diverse editor base collaboratively wrote the book, not a single author. After a long process of discussion and debate, the chapters gradually took on a neutral point of view reached through consensus. Additional editors expanded and contributed to chapters striving to achieve balance and comprehensive coverage. This reduced the regional or cultural bias found in many other books and provided access and breadth on subject matter otherwise little documented.

Char 2C

The **Char 2C** (also known as **FCM 2C**) was a French super-heavy tank developed, although never deployed, during World War I. It was the largest (in physical dimensions) operational tank ever.

Development

In the summer of 1916 General Mouret, the subsecretary of artillery, granted FCM (*Forges et Chantiers de la Mediterranée*), a shipyard in the south of France near Toulon, the contract for the development of a heavy tank. At the time, French industry was very active in lobbying for defence orders, using their connections with high-placed officials and officers to obtain commissions; development contracts could be very profitable even when not resulting in actual production, as they were fully paid for by the state. Mouret's order is puzzling, as the French Army had no stated requirement for a heavy tank, and there was no official policy to procure one. The decision seems to have been purely taken on his personal authority. Exact specifications have been lost, if they ever existed. FCM then largely neglected the project, apart from reaping the financial benefits. At that time all tank projects were highly secret, and thereby shielded from public scrutiny. This was soon to change, however.

On 15 September 1916 the British deployed tanks for the first time in the form of the Mark I, and a veritable tank euphoria followed. When the public mood in Britain had been growing ever darker as the truth of the failure of the Somme Offensive could no longer be suppressed, tanks offered a new hope of final victory. The French people now became curious of the state of their own national tank projects. French politicians, not having been overly involved in them, leaving the matter to the military, were no less inquisitive. This sudden attention greatly alarmed Mouret, who quickly investigated the progress made at FCM and was shocked to find there was none. On 30 September he personally took control of the project. Knowing that the Renault company had some months earlier made several refused proposals to build a heavy tracked mortar, on 12 October he begged Louis Renault to assist FCM in the development of some suitable heavy vehicle. Renault obliged.

Renault consulted his own team that since May 1916 was in the process of designing the revolutionary light Renault FT-17. This work hadn't kept them from considering other tank types, though. Renault, always expecting his employees to provide new ideas instantly, had by this attitude encouraged the team to take a proactive stance, setting a pattern that would last till 1940, and have all kinds of contingency studies ready for the occasion. He discovered that his main designer Rodolphe Ernst-Metzmaier had, by his own initiative, finished a feasibility study for a heavy tank. This fortunate circumstance allowed a wooden full-size mock-up to be quickly constructed and presented to the Consultative Committee of the Assault Artillery on 17 January 1917, after the basic concept had been approved on 30 December. This proposed tank was the most advanced design of its time; it was received very favourably, and a consensus began to form that the project was most promising and a potential "war-winner". It featured a 105 mm gun in a turret, had a proposed weight of 38 tons and 35 mm armour. Even before knowing what the exact nature of the project would be, Mouret had on 20 October ordered one prototype to be built by FCM.

However, the FCM tank had already made a powerful and influential enemy. Brigadier Jean-Baptiste Eugène Estienne, commander of the new tank force, the Assault Artillery, closely cooperated with Renault in the development of the FT-17, and by this connection was kept well informed of the other tank project. Estienne began to fear the production of the heavy vehicle would use up all production facilities, making the procurement of the much more practical light FT-17 impossible. Normally he would have been able to mobilise resistance against it by playing on company rivalries. In this case, though, political pressure could not be exerted this way, as the same industrialist was behind both projects. That his fears were not unfounded became apparent when in November Mouret tried to obstruct the further development of the FT-17, arguing that all available resources should be concentrated into heavy tank production. Alarmed, Estienne now wrote a letter to the Commander-in-Chief, General Joffre on 27 November, defending the light tank concept. In it he admitted that "colossal landships" might in certain circumstances have their uses, but pointed out that, when it was as yet unproven that any workable heavy type could actually be developed, let alone produced in sufficient numbers by French industry, it would be folly not to give priority to light tanks that could be constructed without delay. He insisted that Joffre use all his influence to bring about the cancellation of the heavy tank project.

Joffre answered that Estienne was no doubt correct in his tactical and organisational analysis, but that he couldn't oblige him because political backing of the heavy tank was simply too strong. The Minister of Armament, Albert Thomas, had committed himself too openly to Mouret's cause and now didn't dare to retract from it. Joffre advised Estienne not to worry too much; he would make sure at least the FT-17 wouldn't be cancelled, and precisely because heavy tank development would take such a long time, for the immediate future it wouldn't get in the way of light tank production. There would surely be no harm in allowing some prototypes to be built.

In December Joffre was replaced as supreme commander by Robert Nivelle. In late January Nivelle learned of the heavy tank project from Estienne. He was much more alarmed than Joffre had been. On 29 January he wrote a letter to minister Thomas, making clear that under no circumstances the project could be allowed to impede production of the Schneider CA. Thomas answered on 5 February that there was no danger of this; anyway he had just happened to affirm on 1 February the policy of General Mouret, who — having a great need to show his unrelenting efforts in advancing the cause of the French tank — had ordered the simultaneous development of three prototypes: the lightened "A" version, weighing thirty tons and to be equipped with a 75 mm gun, the "B" version of forty tons with a lengthened hull and two machine gun turrets, and the "C" version of 62 tons with a 105 mm gun and a petro-electrical transmission.

In the spring the Nivelle Offensive failed completely, and the first use of French tanks was likewise a failure; in reaction Thomas ordered all tank production and projects to be ended. This led to an emergency alliance between Estienne and Mouret to bring about a reversal of this decision. When Thomas happened to visit Russia, Mouret surreptitiously ordered a restart of the tank projects. On his return an enraged Thomas caused Mouret to be fired, thus removing Estienne's greatest rival.

In December 1917 the first prototype, the FCM 1A, was ready to be shown to an investigating commission. Mouret had been replaced as head of the commission by Estienne, whose good friend General Philippe Pétain, the new High Commander of the French Army, asked him to use his position to end the project. Estienne told Pétain that this was ill-advised while the public was questioning why these heavy tanks had not been produced. Besides, the allies would only consent to give France 700 Mark VIIIs if France had at least made a token effort to produce its own heavy tanks. They had to delay the project while outwardly endorsing it. Estienne had already set this course by choosing the heaviest version, the "C", for production, requiring a completely new prototype, causing a considerable delay. Then Pétain demanded unreasonably high production numbers, thus delaying planning and initiating a political row.

Pétain asked for 300 heavy tanks to be ready by March 1919, causing a quarrel to erupt between Clemenceau, who was both Prime-Minister and Minister of War, and Louis Loucheur, the Minister of Armament, who felt it was impossible to provide the labour and steel required. Meanwhile, Estienne and Pétain complicated the issue with further demands. Pétain asked for special pontoons, and Estienne demanded battering rams and electronic mine detectors to be fixed. When the war ended, not a single tank had been built.

At first, the production order for the Char 2C was cancelled. Despite the end of hostilities, however, strong political pressure to adopt new heavy tank projects remained, as there was now a considerable surplus capacity in the heavy industry. To stop this, the *Direction de l'Artillerie d'Assaut* on instigation of Estienne decided in April 1919 to procure ten Char 2Cs after all, and use this as an argument to reject any other projects. This wasn't completely successful; even in 1920 it was proposed to the *Section Technique des Appareils de Combat* to build a 600-ton tank with 250 mm armour. At FCM Jammy and Savatier finished the Char 2C prototype, the other nine tanks being built almost simultaneously; all ten were delivered in 1921 and modified by the factory until 1923. They would be the last French tanks to be produced for the home market till the Char D1 pre-series of 1931.

Description

The *Berry*

The Char 2C had a loaded weight of 69 tonnes, partly because of its armour - 45 mm at the front, 22 mm at the sides, but much of it just because of its huge size. The armour was among the thickest of World War I-era tanks, though by modern standards this would be considered thin. It is still easily the largest tank ever taken into production. With the tail fitted, the hull was over twelve metres long. Within its ample frame there was room for two fighting compartments. The first at the front, crowned by a three-man turret (the first in history) with a long 75 mm gun, and the second at the back, topped by a machine gun turret. Both turrets had stroboscopic cupolas. The three independent 8 mm machine gun positions at the front gave protection against infantry assault.

The Char 2C is the only super-heavy tank ever to attain operational status — a super-heavy tank is not simply a tank that is very heavy but one that is much heavier than regular tanks of its period. The next operational tank to weigh about the same would be the Tiger II

heavy tank of World War II.

The fighting compartments were connected by the engine room. Each track was powered by its own 200 or 250 hp engine, via an electrical transmission. Top speed was 15 km/h. Seven fuel tanks, containing 1,260 litres, gave it a range of 150 kilometres.

To man the tank required a crew of twelve: driver, commander, gunner, loader, four machine gunners, mechanic, electrician, assistant-electrician/mechanic and a radio operator. Some sources report thirteen, probably due to pictures of the crews that included the company commander.

Its suspension contains 39 interleaving road wheels on each side, making for a total of 90 wheels on the tank.

Operational history

The ten tanks were part of several consecutive units, their organic strength at one time reduced to three. Their military value slowly decreased as more advanced tanks were developed throughout the 1920s and 1930s. By the end of the 1930s they were largely obsolete, because their slow speed and high profile made them vulnerable to advances in anti-tank guns.

Nevertheless, during the French mobilisation of 1939, all ten were activated and put into their own unit, the 51st *Bataillon de Chars de Combat*. For propaganda, each tank had been named after one of the ancient regions of France, numbers 90-99 named *Poitou; Provence; Picardie; Alsace; Bretagne; Touraine; Anjou; Normandie; Berry; Champagne* respectively. In 1939, the *Normandie* was renamed *Lorraine*. As their main value was in propaganda, the giants were carefully kept from harm and did not participate in the September 1939 attack on the Siegfried Line. They were used for numerous morale-boosting movies, climbing and crushing old French forts instead. To the public, they obtained the reputation of invincible super tanks, the imagined dimensions of which far surpassing the real ones.

Of course, the French commanders knew perfectly well this reputation was undeserved. When the German *Panzer-*

divisionen in the execution of Operation *Fall Rot* ripped apart the French lines after 10 June 1940, the decision was made to prevent the capture of the famous equipment. It was to be sent to the south by rail transport. On 15 June the rail was blocked by a burning fuel train, so it became inevitable to destroy the tanks by detonating charges. Later Goebbels and Goering claimed the tanks were hit by German dive bombers. This propaganda lie was to be repeated by many sources. One tank, the *Champagne*, was nevertheless captured more or less intact and brought to Berlin to be exhibited as a war trophy. In 1948 this tank disappeared, causing many to speculate it still survives at the Russian Tank museum in Kubinka.

Versions

In 1926, the later *Champagne* was modified into the **Char 2C bis**, an experimental type with a 155 mm howitzer in a cast turret. New engines were fitted and the machine gun positions deleted. In this configuration the tank weighed perhaps 74 tons. The change was only temporary though, as the vehicle was brought back into its previous condition the very same year; the new turret was used in the Tunisian Mareth Line.

Between 15 November and 15 December 1939 the *Lorraine*, as the company command tank, was experimentally up-armoured at the *Société des Aciéries d'Homecourt* to make it immune to standard German antitank guns. The front armour was enhanced to 90 mm, the side to 65 mm. In this configuration, weighing about 75 tons, the *Lorraine* had at that time the thickest armour of any operational tank, and is probably still the heaviest operational tank ever.

Replacement

In 1940 12 FCM F1 tanks were ordered, another very large twin-turret tank. France surrendered before they entered service.

Source (edited): "http://en.wikipedia.org/wiki/Char_2C"

Cruiser Mk I

The **Tank, Cruiser, Mk I (A9)** was a British cruiser tank of the interwar period. It was the first cruiser tank: a fast tank designed to bypass the main enemy lines and engage the enemy's lines of communication, along with enemy tanks. The Cruiser Mk II was a heavier armoured adaptation of the Mark I developed at much the same time.

Design and development

In 1936 the British War Office designated two different kinds of tanks for future development: heavily armoured infantry tanks to be used in close cooperation with infantry during attacks, and fast mobile cruiser tanks designed to make forays deep into enemy territory.

In 1934 Sir John Carden of Vickers-Armstrong had produced a new medium tank, the A9, which was subsequently designated the Cruiser Tank Mark I. It incorporated the best features of the earlier Mk III Light Tank, and was powered by a commercial petrol engine. However, this was still in the time of the Great depression and the tank had a number of cost-cutting measures applied. It was the first British tank to have a centrally-located turret, but was poorly armoured, with a maximum of 14 mm thickness, many armour faces were vertical, and there were numerous shot traps.

The driver's compartment and the fighting compartments were not separated. As well as the turret armament, which consisted of a QF 2-pounder (40 mm) gun and a coaxial Vickers machine gun, there were two small turrets either side of the driver's compartment, each sporting one more machine-gun. Both these smaller turrets were permanently manned, which gave the tank a total crew of 6 (Commander, gunner, loader, driver and two machine-gunners).

The tank entered testing in 1936 and 125 were ordered in the summer of 1937 as an interim design pending the delivery of a Cruiser tank based on the Christie suspension. 75 were built by Harland and Wolff, and the other 50 were built by Vickers. Originally a Rolls-Royce car engine was used, but this proved underpowered and was replaced by an AEC bus engine.

The later Valentine Infantry tank essentially used the same lower hull and suspension, though with considerably more armour.

The A9 weighed 12 tons, was 5.8 metres long, 2.65 metres high, 2.5 metres wide, and had a top speed of 25 mph on road and 15 mph off. Its maximum road range was 150 miles. The ammunition load was 100 2-pounder rounds and a total of 3,000 rounds for the three Vickers machine guns.

Service

A damaged Cruiser Mk I CS abandoned in Calais, 1940.

The Cruiser was an effective tank in the French, Greek and early North African campaigns. The 2 pdr gun was lethal against the early Italian tanks encountered during the North African campaign and could hold its own against Rommel's early Panzer IIs and IIIs. The A9's 2-pounder gun could also breach the 20 – 30 mm of protective steel on later opponents such as the Panzer III varient D and the Panzer IV D. It was effective until the Germans introduced the more thickly armoured Panzer IV E varient to the desert in Spring 1941. However, the minimal armour made the A9 an easy kill for most Axis anti-tank weapons. Also problematic was the lack of High Explosive shells for the 2 pdr gun and even worse the lack of AP for the 95 mm gun on the Close Support version. Another issue was that the areas around the front machine gun turrets created a frontal surface that was more vulnerable to enemy fire than it would have been had it been a flat plate, let alone a sloped glacis.

The mechanical unreliability of the Cruiser was also a disadvantage. In particular, tracks were easily slewed causing difficulties.

Variants

Mark I (A9)

Used by the 1st Armoured Division in the Battle of France (1940). Used by the 2nd and 7th Armoured Divisions in North Africa until 1941.

Mark I CS

Had a 3.7 inch (94 mm) /L15 howitzer installed in the turret. This gun only fired smoke rounds, 40 of which were carried.

See also

- Cruiser tank
- List of tanks of the United Kingdom

Notes

References

- Tucker, Spencer (2004). *Tanks: An Illustrated History of Their Impact.* ABC-CLIO. pp. 49–51. ISBN 1576079953.
- Forty, George; Jack Livesy (2006). *The World Encyclopedia of Tanks & Armoured Fighting Vehicles.* Lorenz Books. pp. 55. ISBN 9780754817.
- WWIIvehicles.com, accessed 23 October 2007

External links

- A9 Specifications at OnWar.com

Source (edited): "http://en.wikipedia.org/wiki/Cruiser_Mk_I"

FCM F1

The **FCM F1** was a French super-heavy tank developed during the Interbellum by the *Forges et Chantiers de la Méditerranée* company. Twelve were ordered in 1940 to replace the Char 2C, but France was defeated before construction could begin, a wooden mock-up being all that was finished. The FCM F1 was large and elongated, and had two turrets: one in front and one in the back, with a single high-velocity gun in each turret. The rear turret was higher so it could shoot over the first one. The vehicle was intended to be heavily armoured. Its size and protection level made it early 1940 with about 140 tons the heaviest tank actually ordered. Despite two engines its speed would have been slow. The primary purpose of the tank was to breach German fortification lines, not to fight enemy tanks. The development path of the FCM F1 was extremely complex, due to the existence of a number of parallel super-heavy tank projects with overlapping design goals, the specifications of which were regularly changed. For each project again several companies submitted one or more competing proposals.

The *Char Lourd*

In the twenties France used a typology of tanks, classified according to weight. The heaviest class was formed by the *Char Lourd*, or "heavy tank". In the programmes of 1921 and 1930, no new tank was foreseen for this class, the Char 2C fulfilling the role of *Char Lourd*. The programme of 1926 led in 1928 to a *Char d'Arrêt* project of fifty tons; when conceptual studies by FCM had reached 100 tons, in February 1929 a new plan for a somewhat lighter 65 ton vehicle was started but terminated on 17 May 1929 for budgetary reasons.

On 4 May 1936 however, the *Conseil Consulatif de l'Armement* under General Julien Claude Marie Sosthène Dufieux decided to develop a new heavy tank, with the following specifications given on 12 November 1936: a maximum weight of 45 metric tons, immunity to 75 mm AP fire above 200 metres, a speed of 30 km/h, a range of 200 kilometres and an armament consisting of a long 75 mm gun in the hull and a 47 mm gun in a turret. It would thus have resembled an oversized Char B1, of which tank several other development projects were ongoing.

In 1937 three manufacturers, AMX, ARL and FCM, presented prototype proposals; ARL even three of them. All of these however had already a higher projected weight than 45 tons — and threatened to become even heavier during actual construction. In reaction it was first decided by the *Conseil Supérieur de la Guerre* on 26 March 1937 to build a very small and cheap but heavily armoured (60 mm) vehicle instead, on the lines of the British Matilda I. The first designs featured a 37 mm gun. When a better armament was demanded, it was understood through a study by the *Section de l'Armement et des Études Techniques* (SAET) on 5 April 1937 that the tank would still weigh a twenty tons, while another tank, the Char G1, was already in development in this weight class. As a result in February 1938 the specifications were again radically changed and now asked for a superheavy tank with a 75 mm gun in a turret; no weight limits were imposed. The new specifications were closest to the original FCM proposal of sixty tons and so the French Supreme Command decided on 6 April 1938 to grant FCM a development contract for a **Char F1**. It was realised however that this project could be no more than an intermediate step in heavy tank design and already a special commission had been formed in February, headed by the inspector-general of tanks, Julien François René Martin, to further study the problem of overcoming the new defences of the *Westwall* being at the time constructed on the western German border.

The *Char d'Attaque des Fortifications*

The commission immediately revived the *Char Lourd* concept but applied it only to the "45 ton tank" project and differentiated this from a tank optimised for destroying modern fortifications, a *Char d'Attaque des Fortifications*. This latter vehicle should have a powerful high velocity gun in a turret but be itself immune to enemy antitank-guns. Speed was considered of secondary import and might be as low as 10 km/h maximum. However trench-crossing and wading abilities would have to be excellent. If this should result in an overly cumbersome vehicle, it should be made modular so that the components could be transported separately. On 4 May 1938 the *Direction des Fabrications d'Armement* proposed to call this the *Char H* project, to distinguish it from the *Char F*, but this was rejected as there was some danger of confusion with the Hotchkiss H35.

The French High Command approved of the plans of the commission in April 1938 and now appointed a second commission to work them out in detail. This new commission should also consider the question of whether a 45 ton vehicle might not after all be sufficient. In its first meeting on 9 May 1938, the commission quickly came to the conclusion that to meet the tactical demands a 75 mm gun in a turret was necessary and 120 mm armour allround. This could not be reconciled with a weight of 45 tons. On the other hand to equal the climbing and crossing mobility of even the old Char 2C would likely result in a 150-200 ton behemoth, of which even the modules would be impractical to transport. It was therefore decided to further research the possibility of a 65 ton vehicle, with an empty hull weight of 45 tons.

In its second meeting on 22 July 1938, some troubling data were considered. Most bridges could carry a maximum single vehicle load of 35 tons, so the new tank would have to cross rivers on special pontoons. German tank moats transpired to have a width of about seven metres, so a very long vehicle seemed to be necessary. Existing rail road cars could carry a maximum of 100 tons though. It was also pointed out that 120 mm armour might not be enough in view of the powerful German 88 mm gun. The commission rejected the *char minimum* proposal of 56 tons as it had insufficient trench-crossing capacity. It also discarded a proposal by engineer Boirault to build a futuristic 120 ton articulated tank. It retained two options: the *char maximum* of 89 tons, demountable in two sections, and the *char squelette* of 110 tons and a trench-crossing ability of eight metres, on the general lines of the World War I American Skeleton Tank, but with the added feature that the main body could move in relation to the skeleton track frame in order to shift its point of gravity.

In September 1938 the Supreme Command ordered to immediately start research into both possibilities. The ARL company was granted a development contract for the *char maximum*, the first proposal for which was presented by ARL in May 1939. It had a proposed weight of 120 tons, consisted of two detachable modules and could be armed by either a gun or a flamethrower. The commission decided that only the guntank would be considered, but that a second turret at the back was needed for defence against infantry assault. It also remarked that the project was quite similar to that of the Char F1 and that perhaps both programmes should be merged.

Second World War

September 1939 Programme

When the Second World War broke out in September 1939 some hurried measures were taken to have an operational heavy tank ready for the planned offensive against Germany in 1941, even though the French High Command did not have great faith in the super-heavy tank project and intended to circumvent the *Westwall* by violating the neutrality of the Low Countries, should these refuse to join the Entente in time. The skeleton tank, being too futuristic, was abandoned. Despite the hurry, the lack of real progress made did not allow for a concentration of all effort into a single design, as it was still unclear whether a working prototype could be provided in time. Three companies, FCM, ARL and AMX, were therefore in October ordered to construct two different prototypes each, for a total of six models. These should fit existing railway wagons, which the F1 did not. The flamethrower option should be abandoned.

On 22 December 1939 more precise specifications were made. FCM should complete the F1 with a 75 mm gun but also build a F1 hull with a 90 or 105 mm gun in the superstructure, because the 75 mm gun was likely too weak. As the Char F1 was designed with 100 mm armour, this should be enhanced on the front to 120 mm. A secondary turret with a 47 mm gun should protect the back. Both AMX and ARL should build prototypes with 105 and 90 mm guns in a turret — the turrets themselves being independently designed, as usual for French tanks — and a secondary turret with a 47 mm gun. That month both FCM and ARL indicated that they expect to begin construction of the prototypes in the summer of 1940 and series production at the end of 1941; for AMX it was too soon to make any precise predictions. ARL on 17 January 1940 ordered four turrets from the Schneider company, but it agreed only to build two 105 mm gun turrets and refuses the two 90 mm gun turrets, as there was simply no capacity to manufacture them.

In February 1940 the *Société d'Études et d'Application Mécanique* (SEAM) proposed a tank designed by the Polish engineer Prince André Poniatowski. It was a truly gigantic vehicle, weighing 220 tons, to be moved by two Hispano engines of 925 hp each, via a petro-electrical transmission. The project tried to recommend itself by pointing out that the hull was over five meters wide while being only twelve metres long and thus had a superior length-width ratio, facilitating steering. For transport the vehicle could be split in two sides along its entire length. Unsurprisingly on 20 April 1940 it was refused by the Ministry of Defence.

On 4 March 1940 a new subcommission to supervise the heavy tank design learned that the 90 and 105 mm gun turret designs were ready, i.e. on paper. It decided to abandon the AMX projects as they were hopelessly behind schedule; its *Tracteur C* could not be ready before July 1941. AMX terminated development on 1 April. The subcommission advised to go ahead with both the FCM F1 and the ARL prototypes and already order ten or fifteen of the former. That advice was given to a new overarching Commission of Tank Study, to which ARL presented a wooden mock-up on 11 April 1940 and FCM one on the day after. It transpired that the FCM project was far more advanced and could show the new tank in every detail. The design had a sloped armour front plate, a small turret in front, instead of behind as specified, and a higher turret at the back, able to hold a 90 mm gun instead of the specified 75 mm gun. The tank had a projected weight of 140 metric tons, to be moved at 24 km/h by two 550 hp Renault engines via an electrical transmission. The Commission decided to abandon the ARL projects and make a preliminary order for twelve FCM F1s, to be delivered from May 1941 onward at three or four tanks a month. This expectation to have some tanks ready for the summer of 1941 was a very important consideration, as the entire heavy tank project faced strong opposition from those who see it as a waste of scarce resources, better spent on building more Char B1s. The Commission also asked FCM to bring the armour protection to 120 mm all-round, though this would increase weight to 145 tons and reduce maximum speed to 20 km/h. For the commission this was a departure from its earlier decisions about a future *Char de Forteresse*.

The *Char de Forteresse*

On 28 February 1940 a new commission for the study of tank design was established, the *Commission d'Études des Chars*, to create a coherent policy for future French tank production. The commission planned for three weight classes, the heaviest of which was the *Char de Forteresse*. This tank was envisaged as a sort of "Super Char B" with a 135 or 155 mm howitzer in the hull and a 75 or 90 mm gun in the turret. Its armour should be 100 or 120 mm all-round. Nevertheless its weight was very optimistically expected to be around 80-100 tons, powered by a 1000 hp engine. On 14 May it was decided that, there being no suitable 135 or 155 mm gun available, the project would be dropped.

Aftermath

After the Fall of France all official design on heavy tanks was halted. The Char F1 showed quite a few similarities though to the ARL 44, produced just after the war. In 1944 the Allies had developed some new vehicles with exactly the same purpose as the FCM F1: to breach the Siegfried Line. The British had the Tortoise heavy assault tank, the Americans the T-28 Super Heavy Tank. Both designs were self-propelled guns however, not multi-turreted tanks, allowing them to be lighter and still better protected. Like the FCM 1 they would not be taken into production.

Source (edited): "http://en.wikipedia.org/wiki/FCM_F1"

Medium Mark III

The **Medium Mark III** was a medium tank developed in the United Kingdom during the inter-war period. The tank was unsuccessful with only 3 built. The design did not directly derive from earlier Medium Mark II tank.

Development history

A6 "Sixteen tonners"

In 1926, the British War Office wanted to replace their existing Mark II tanks with a new design. In May the Royal Tank Corps Centre was asked for its opinion, which it submitted in July. One of the requirements was a weight limit of 15.5 tons, which led to the nickname "16-tonners". Other specifications included that it could transported by rail; a sufficient supply of lubrication oil to match the range of the tank (dictated by the fuel carried); a wireless set; a gun capable of defeating enemy armour at a range of at least a thousand yards; fuel tanks external to the main compartments and bottom armour sufficient to withstand heavy machine-gun fire when exposed while climbing a crest. Furthermore the machine should be as silent as possible, as with previous types the engine noise tended to incapacitate the crew.

The War Office added some extra requirements: a separate engine compartment; superior steering capacity and 13 millimetres frontal armour with 9 millimetres thickness for the other plates.

In September Vickers, given the order to build a prototype, proposed a first design based on the Vickers A1E1 Independent, with the fighting compartment in front and the engine compartment at the back. There would be a central two-man turret with a 3-pounder (47 mm) gun and a coaxial machine-gun; it was intended to house the commander and a special observer, each being provided a separate cupola. In the front of the hull were to be placed two secondary machine-gun turrets, each with a twin Vickers machine gun. At the back of the vehicle, behind the main turret a third machine-gun turret was intended, armed with an anti-aircraft (AA) weapon. A crew was needed of seven men. Maximum armour would be 13 millimetres and basis armour 6.5 millimetres, limiting the weight to fourteen tons. Riveted plates were used. The total fuel supply would be 120 imp gal (550 l) gallons: ten in a small tank inside, gravity feeding the engine; the remainder in external tanks on the fenders. Two engine options were indicated: a 120 hp engine would allow for a speed of 14 mph and a 180 hp engine would raise this to 20 mph (32 km/h).

The result was called **A6**. In March 1927 a wooden mock-up was presented and after approval a second and prototype were ordered which had to incorporate the new hydraulically operated Wilson epicyclic steering gearbox, the predecessor of the Merrit-Brown gearbox. By June 1928 both prototypes (A6E1 and A6E2) were presented to the Mechanised Warfare Experimental Establishment for trials. Vickers was on this occasion ordered to add armour skirts but keep within the weight limit by removing armour elsewhere. Meanwhile a third prototype had been ordered: A6E3.

A6E1 and A6E3 were fitted with a Armstrong Siddeley air-cooled V8 180 hp engine giving a maximum speed of 26 mph; A6E2 however, originally with the Ricardo CI 180 hp engine. Later A6E3 was re-engined with the Thornycroft 6V 500 hp. It was proposed to combine two Rolls-Royce Phantom engines with the Wilson transmission system on the A6E1, but in view of the costs this was rejected. A6E2 was eventually refitted with the AS V8 180 hp.

The guns were tested in July 1928. This proved that the twin-machine gun arrangement was unworkable; the A6E3, then being constructed, therefore was fitted with a simplified design with a single machine-gun; it also had single cupola on the centreline of the turret. The AA-turret was removed from A6E1. However it was also shown that the suspension and the gunnery arrangements were distinctly inferior to those of the Mark II. It was therefore decided to discontinue the development of the type and use the three vehicles merely as test-beds for the automotive parts. In 1929 Vickers submitted three alternative suspension designs, which were fitted to the respective prototypes; one of these, tried on A6E3, involved a fundamental reconstruction of the hull. None proved able to provide a stable gun platform. Only in 1934 a satisfactory type was fitted by a specialised firm.

Medium Mark III

A Medium III in use as a command vehicle

The disappointments in the A6 design led to a new design, the "Medium Mark III", being ordered in 1928 and constructed from 1930. It was similar to the A6 design but featured a new turret and improved armour. The turret had a flat gun mantlet and a bulge at the back to hold the radio set. The secondary machine-gun turrets were moved more to the front to shift the centre of gravity of the entire vehicle forward to improve its stability. Larger brakes were fitted. In 1933 trials were completed of the first two prototypes. The type was reliable and provided a good gun platform. However, it still suffered from its bad suspension design: even though road speed increased to thirty miles per hour, during cross-country rides the bogies were often overloaded. Three Mark IIIs were built, one by Vickers and two by the Royal Ordnance Factory at Woolwich: Medium III E1, E2 and E3. The third had an improved suspension and the vehicles were in 1934 taken into use by the HQ of the Tank Brigade. However, no orders followed due to its high price; Medium III E2 was lost to a fire. Source (edited): "http://en.wikipedia.org/wiki/Medium_Mark_III"

Neubaufahrzeug

The German **Neubaufahrzeug** series of tank prototypes were a first attempt to create a heavy tank for the Wehrmacht after Adolf Hitler had come to power. Multi-turreted, heavy and slow, they did not fit in with the Blitzkrieg tactics and therefore only five were made. These were primarily used for propaganda purposes, though three took part in the Battle of Norway in 1940.

Development

Neubaufahrzeug under construction

During the 1920's and 1930's, a number of countries experimented with very large, multi-turreted tanks. The British built a single example of the Vickers A1E1 Independent in 1926. This inspired the Soviet T-35, which was built in limited numbers from 1933.

Development of the Neubaufahrzeug (German for "new construction vehicle") started in 1933 when the then Reichswehr gave a contract for the development of a *Großtraktor* (heavy tractor) to both Rheinmetall and Krupp. *Grosstractor* was a codename for the development of a heavy tank, Germany being still forbidden to develop tanks under the terms of the Treaty of Versailles.

The two designs resembled each other to a great extent, the main difference being the weapons placement. Each had a main turret armed with a 75 mm KwK L/24 main gun and secondary 37 mm KwK L/45. Rheinmetall's design mounted the second gun above the 75 mm KwK L/24, while the Krupp design had it mounted next to the 75 mm KwK L/24. Both designs had a secondary turret mounted to the front and the rear of the main turret. These turrets were slightly adapted Panzer I turrets, with the standard machinegun armament.

Rheinmetall's design was designated the PzKpfw NbFz V ('PanzerKampfwagen NeubauFahrzeug V'), and the Krupp design the PzKpfw NbFz VI. It was intended that these designs would fulfill the role of heavy tank in the armored forces, but the design proved to be too complex and unreliable for this role. Development nevertheless continued in order for the nascent German military to gain experience with multi-turreted tanks.

In 1934 Rheinmetall built two mild steel prototypes, both with their own turret design. Three more prototypes were built with proper armor and the Krupp turret in 1935 and 1936.

Combat history

Three Neubaufahrzeuge arriving in Oslo Harbour, April 1940

Though these tanks were never placed in production, they provided a propaganda tool for Nazi Germany, for example being shown at the International Automobile Exposition in Berlin in 1939.

This propaganda role was extended with the German invasion of Norway, when a special *Panzerabteilung* was formed which took the three armored prototypes with them to Oslo. They saw some combat there, with one being blown up by German engineers when it got stuck in swamps near Åndalsnes. To replace it, one of the mild steel prototypes was used.

It is unclear what happened to the tanks after the Norway campaign, but none of them survived the war. The surviving vehicles were ordered scrapped in 1941, which took place in 1942 according to documents captured by the British in 1945. The dates upon which the vehicles were scrapped are unclear,

SMK tank

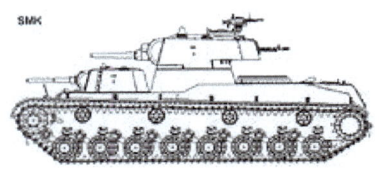

SMK (Sergius Mironovitch Kirov) was an armored vehicle prototype developed by the Soviet Union prior to the Second World War. The SMK was also known to German intelligence as the T-35C.

History

The SMK was among the designs competing to replace the unreliable and expensive T-35.

The testing ground for the SMK and other competing models, which included the KV-1, was the Winter War. The KV-1 design was chosen due to its resistance against Finnish anti-tank weapons.

Source (edited): "http://en.wikipedia.org/wiki/SMK_tank"

T-100 tank

The **T-100** was a twin-turreted Soviet heavy tank prototype, designed in 1938–39, which led to the development of the Kliment Voroshilov tank (KV-1). The T-100 was designed to be a superheavy breakthrough tank by N. Barykov's OKMO design team at S.M. Kirov Factory No. 185 in Leningrad.

The project was initiated by the Red Army's need to replace the aging five-turreted T-35 tank based on combat experience in the Spanish Civil War. One of the lessons the Red Army drew from this conflict was the need for heavy 'shell-proof' armor on medium and heavy tanks. Although the T-35 was never used in Spain, its thin armor was vulnerable to the small towed antitank guns and gun-armed tanks encountered there by Soviet T-26 and BT tanks.

The T-100 was in direct competition against the very similar SMK heavy tank, by Lt-Col Zh. Kotin's team at the Leningrad Kirovsky Factory. The original specification was for a five-turreted "anti-tank gun destroyer" which would resist 37mm guns at any range and 76.2mm guns at 1,200 m. Both design teams objected to the antiquated multi-turreted design, and the requirement was reduced to two turrets before serious design work began. Both tanks had some modern features, including thick, welded armor, radios, and torsion bar suspension.

The T-100 tank sported two turrets placed on a very long chassis. The front turret, mounting a 45mm antitank gun, was placed at a lower elevation than the other, thus giving the front turret a limited area of fire. The top turret, mounting a 76.2mm gun, was able to turn a full 360 degrees. The multi-turret design concept had been common in the 1930s, reaching its extreme with the British Vickers A1E1 Independent and the Soviets' own derivative T-35.

Kotin received permission to enter a third design into the competition, the single-turreted KV tank, was much more modern, with a single large turret housing a dual-purpose gun.

The prototype T-100 tank was briefly tested in the Soviet invasion of Finland in 1939 without success. It was never put into production, due to the archaic design concept, poor mobility, and the availability of a far superior alternative, the KV series. It did lead to the SU-100Y self-propelled gun, which did not go into production, although the prototype was used in the defence of Moscow in 1941.

Source (edited): "http://en.wikipedia.org/wiki/T-100_tank"

T-24 tank

The **T-24** was a Soviet medium tank built in 1931. Only twenty-four tanks were built, and saw no combat. This was the first tank produced at the KhPZ factory in Ukraine, which was later responsible for the very successful T-34 and T-54 Soviet tanks. The T-24's suspension was used successfully in the Soviet Union's first purpose-built artillery tractors.

The T-24's main armament was a 45 mm gun. It had a ball-mount 7.62 mm DT machine gun in the hull, another in the turret, and a third in a secondary turret atop the main turret. The tank was well-armoured for its time, but suffered from problems with the engine and transmission.

Production history

A tank design bureau was established at the Kharkov Locomotive Factory (KhPZ) in Kharkiv, Soviet Ukraine, in 1928. The first tank project of the factory was the T-12 (or T-1-12). This was a larger version of the T-18, with a more powerful engine (the T-18 was based on the Renault FT-17). One prototype was built and production of thirty tanks in 1930 was authorized, but automotive performance was so disappointing that it was decided to do further development work.

The project was re-designated T-24, work was completed fixing problems with the transmission and fuel system, and a larger turret was designed. Initial trials were conducted, during which performance was found satisfactory, although the prototype's engine caught fire, and the turret had to be transferred to a T-12 prototype for further testing. Only a total of twenty-four were built during 1931. The T-24s were originally armed only with machine guns, until the 45 mm guns were installed in the following year.

The T-24 was found unreliable, and was used only for training and parades. Although the T-24 tank was a failure, it gave the KhPZ its initial tank design and production experience, which was applied much more successfully in adopting production of the U.S. Christie tank as the BT tank series, starting in 1931.

Artillery tractors

Voroshilovets heavy artillery tractor

Komintern artillery tractor

The KhPZ's *Komintern* artillery tractor was based on the suspension of the T-12 tank (50 built from 1930) and later the T-24 (2,000 built from 1935 to 1941), powered by a 131-hp diesel engine. Despite the dismal fate of its predecessor tanks, the tractor was more successful and was put into mass production. The *Komintern* inherited several of the T-24's disadvantages, but some of them were fixed by designers, others were not as significant for tractor as for a tank. The *Komintern* was used to tow medium artillery such as the 152 mm gun-howitzer.

The **Voroshilovets heavy artillery tractor** was also based on the T-24's suspension, using the same Model V-2 diesel engine as the BT-7M and T-34 tanks. About 230 were built at KhPZ from 1939, and after the German invasion of 1941 production was shifted to the Stalingrad Tractor Factory until August 1942.

References

- Zaloga, Steven J.; James Grandsen (1984). *Soviet Tanks and Combat Vehicles of World War Two*. London: Arms and Armour Press. ISBN 0-85368-606-8.

External links

- Komintern at battlefield.ru
- T-12, T-24, Komintern, Voroshilovets at KMDB design bureau's official site
- T-24 Medium Tank at battlefield.ru
- Первые советские танки (First Soviet tanks), at M. Svirin's *Soviet Tanks*, in Russian
- Первые Средние (First Mediums), from *Modelist-Konstruktor*, no 9, 1989, in Russian

Source (edited): "http://en.wikipedia.org/wiki/T-24_tank"

T-26

The **T-26** tank was a Soviet light infantry tank used during many conflicts of the 1930s as well as during World War II. It was a development of the British Vickers 6-Ton tank and is widely considered one of the most successful tank designs of the 1930s.

It was produced in greater numbers than any other tank of the period, with more than 11,000 produced. During the 1930s, the USSR developed approximately 53 variants of the T-26, including other combat vehicles based on its chassis. Twenty-three of these were mass-produced.

The T-26 was used extensively in the armies of Spain, China and Turkey. In addition, captured T-26 light tanks were used by the Finnish, German, Romanian and Hungarian armies.

Though nearly obsolete by the beginning of World War II, the T-26 was the most important tank of the Spanish Civil War and played a significant role during the Battle of Lake Khasan in 1938 as well as in the Winter War in 1939-40. The T-26 was the most numerous tank in the Red Army's armored force during the German invasion of the Soviet Union in June 1941. The Soviet T-26 light tanks last saw use in August 1945, during the Soviet invasion of Manchuria.

The T-26 was reliable and simple to maintain, and its design was continually modernised between 1931 and 1941. However, no new models of the T-26 were developed after 1940.

British origin

The T-26 was a Soviet development of the British Vickers 6-Ton (Vickers Mk.E) light tank, which was designed by the Vickers-Armstrongs Company in 1928-1929. The simple and easy to maintain Vickers 6-Ton was intended especially for export to less technically advanced countries: the Soviet Union, Poland, Brazil, Argentina, Japan, Thailand, China and many others. Vickers advertised the tank in military publications, and both the Soviet Union and Poland expressed interest in the Vickers design.

In spring 1930, the Soviet buying committee, under the direction of Semyon Ginzburg, arrived in Great Britain to select tanks, tractors and cars to be used in the Red Army. The Vickers 6-Ton was among four models of tanks selected by Soviet representatives during their visit to the Vickers-Armstrongs Company. According to the contract signed on May 28, 1930, the company delivered to the USSR 15 twin-turreted Vickers Mk.E (Type A, armed with two .303 calibre (7.7 mm) water-cooled Vickers machine guns) tanks together with full technical documentation to enable series production of the tank in the USSR. The ability of the two turrets of the Type A to turn independently made it possible to fire to both the left and right at once, which was considered advantageous for breakthroughs of field entrenchments. Several Soviet engineers participated in assembly of the tanks at the Vickers Factory in 1930.

The first four Vickers 6-Ton tanks arrived in the USSR at the end of 1930. The last tanks did not arrive until 1932, when series production of the T-26 was already in progress. The British tanks were issued to Soviet factories for study in preparation for series production and to military educational institutions and training units. Later, some tanks were given to military supply depots and proving grounds.

The Vickers-built 6-Ton tanks had the designator V-26 in the USSR. Three British tanks were successfully tested for cross-country ability at the small proving ground near Moscow on Poklonnaya Hill in January 1931. One tank hull was tested for gunfire resistance in August 1931. Kliment Voroshilov ordered the creation of the "Special Commission for the Red Army (RKKA) new tanks" under the direction of S. Ginzburg to define the tank type suitable for the Red Army. The T-19 8-ton light infantry tank, developed by S. Ginzburg under that programme at the *Bolshevik* Factory in Leningrad was a theoretical competitor to the British Vickers 6-Ton. The first prototype of the complex and expensive T-19 was not finished until August 1931. Because both tanks had advantages and disadvantages, S. Ginzburg suggested developing a more powerful, hybrid tank (the so called "improved" T-19) with the hull, home-developed engine and armament from the native T-19, and the transmission and chassis from the British Vickers 6-ton.

However, on January 26, 1931, I. Khalepsky (chief of the Department of Mechanisation and Motorisation of the RKKA) wrote a letter to S. Ginzburg with information obtained via the intelligence service that the Polish government had decided to purchase Vickers 6-Ton light infantry tanks as well as Christie cavalry tanks and to mass produce them with the assistance of both the British and French. Because Poland was then considered, in Soviet military doctrine, to be the USSR's main enemy, the Soviet Revolutionary Military Council took this erroneous information into consideration and decided to pass the aforementioned foreign tanks into Red Army service immediately in order to counter possible aggression. At that time, the RKKA had only several dozen outdated Mk.V, Mk.A and Renault FT-17 tanks, captured during the Russian Civil War, together with various armoured cars and obsolescent domestic MS-1 (T-18) light infantry tanks. On February 13, 1931, the Vickers 6-Ton light infantry tank, under the designator T-26, officially entered service in the Red Army as the "main tank for close support of combined arms units and tank units of High Command reserve"

One of the Vickers 6-Ton tanks (equipped with Soviet-made turrets for the T-26) was tested for gunfire resistance in August 1931. The hull was subjected to rifle and Maxim machine gun fire with the use of normal and armour-piercing bullets at a range of 50 m (160 ft). It was found that the armour withstood gunfire with minimal damage (only some rivets were damaged). Chemical analysis showed that the front armour plates were made from high-quality cemented armour (S.t.a Plat according to Vickers-Armstrongs class fication), whereas the homogeneous roof and bottom armour plates were made from mediocre steel. Nevertheless, the British armour was better than armour produced by Izhora Factory for the first T-26s due to a shortage of modern metallurgical equipment in the USSR that time.

The prototype of TMM-1 light infantry tank during tests in spring 1932.

At the same time, the Faculty of Mechanisation and Motorisation of the Military Technical Academy named after F.E. Dzerzhinsky developed two tank models (TMM-1 and TMM-2) based on the purchased Vickers 6-Ton tank design but with an American Hercules 95 hp (71 kW) six-cylinder water-cooled engine, improved front armour (to 15–20 mm), and a driver's position on the left side. TMM stands for *tank maloy moshchnosti* or "tank of low power". The TMM-1 was equipped with transmission details from the Ya-5 truck and a ball mount for the DT tank machine gun in front of the hull, whereas the TMM-2 was equipped with an improved gear box, a steering device without clutches and a 37 mm Hotchkiss gun in the right turret. However, representatives from the main Soviet tank manufacturers together with officials from the RKKA Mobilization Department considered the Hercules engine to be too difficult to produce, and the engine tended to overheat inside the engine compartment. Tests of TMM-1 and TMM-2 prototypes performed in the beginning of 1932 demonstrated no advantage over the Vickers 6-Ton and the T-26 (the TMM-2's maneuverability was found to be even worse).

Design

Maintenance of the T-26 mod. 1931 (with riveted hull and turrets). This tank was produced in the first half of 1932 - note the mounting of exhaust muffler with two clamps and the cover over the air outlet window. The Moscow Military District. Summer 1934.

The Soviets did not simply replicate the Vickers Six-Ton. Like its British counterpart, the T-26 mod. 1931 had a twin-turreted configuration and was designed to carry two machine guns, mounting one in each turret. A major difference between the Soviet T-26 mod. 1931 and the British 6-Ton were higher turrets on the T-26, complete with observation slit. Also Soviet turrets had a round firing port for the DT tank machine gun, as opposed to the rectangular ports used by the original British design for the Vickers machine gun. The front part of the hull was also slightly modified.

Hulls of twin-turreted T-26s were assembled using armoured plates riveted to a frame from metal angles. Some tanks, produced in 1931, had sealing zinc shims at the hull bottom at the interface between armoured plates for fording water obstacles. After experiencing problems with precipitation entering the engine compartment, a special cover was installed over an air outlet window after March 1932. A number of T-26s produced at the end of 1932-1933 had a riveted and welded hull. The T-26 mod. 1931 had two cylindrical turrets mounted on ball bearings; each turret turned independently through 240°. Both turrets could provide common fire in front and rear arcs of fire (100° each). The disadvantage of such configuration was impossibility to use all tank fire-power at once on the same side. Four technological modifications of turrets existed, and they were mounted on tanks in different combinations (for instance, a tank with a riveted hull could have riveted and welded turrets).

The hull and turrets of the T-26 mod. 1931 had a maximum armour thickness of 13-15 mm, which was sufficient to withstand a light machine gun fire. Nevertheless, many twin-turreted tanks of the first series had 10 mm armour plates of low quality, which could be penetrated by 7.62 mm armour-piercing bullets from 150 m. In 1938, the T-26 was upgraded to the model 1938 version which had a new conical turret with better anti-bullet resistance but the same welded hull as the T-26 mod. 1933 produced in 1935-1936. This proved insufficient in the Battle of Lake Khasan, which took place in 1938, so the tank was upgraded once more in February 1939 to have an underturret box with sloped (23°) 20 mm side armoured plates. The turret featured an increase to 20 mm at 18 degrees sloping. This time it was designated T-26-1 (known as the T-26 mod. 1939 in modern sources). There would be subsequent attempts to thicken the front plate, but T-26 production soon ended in favor of other designs, such as the T-34.

In 1933, the Soviets unveiled the T-26 mod. 1933. The Model 1933, with a new single cylindrical turret carrying one 45 mm cannon and one 7.62 mm machine gun, would become the most common T-26 variant. The 45 mm 20K tank gun was based on the German Pak 35/36 cannon acquired in 1930. The T-26 could carry up to three secondary DT 7.62 mm machine guns in coaxial, rear, and anti-aircraft mounts. This increased fire-power was intended to aid crews in defeating dedicated anti-tank teams, as the original machine gun armament had been found insufficient. The turret rear ball mounting for the additional DT tank machine gun was installed on the T-26 tanks from the end of 1935 until 1939.

Interior of T-26 mod. 1933 turret. Left-side ammunition stowage. Note the side observation device and the porthole for revolver which closed with a plug. Parola Tank Museum in Finland.

Interior of T-26 mod. 1933 turret, looking forward at the 45 mm 20K tank gun breech. Note the TOP-1 telescopic sight to the left, the coaxial DT tank machine gun and PT-K commander panoramic sight to the right. Parola Tank Museum in Finland.

The T-26 Model 1933 carried 122 rounds of 45 mm ammunition, firing armour-piercing 45 mm rounds with a muzzle velocity of 820 m/s (2,700 ft/s), or lower-velocity high-explosive munitions. Tanks intended for company commanders were equipped with a radio set and a hand-rail radio antenna on the turret. Later the hand-rail antenna was replaced with a buggy-whip antenna, because the Spanish Civil War and Battle of Lake Khasan demonstrated that the hand-rail antenna unmasked commander tanks for enemy fire.

The tank was powered by a T-26 90 hp (67 kW) flat row 4-cylinder air-cooled petrol engine which represented a Soviet full copy of the Armstrong Siddeley engine used in the Vickers 6-Ton. The engine was located in the rear part of the hull. In the beginning, Soviet-made tank engines were of bad quality; they were improved beginning in 1934. The T-26 (Armstrong Siddeley) engine did not have an over-speed limiter, which often resulted in overheating and engine valve breakage, especially in summer. A fuel tank for 182 L (40 imp gal, 48 U.S. gal) and an oil box for 27 L (5.9 imp gal; 7.1 U.S. gal) were placed alongside of the engine. The engine required top-grade petrol; the use of second-rate petrol could cause damage to the valve units because of engine detonation. From mid 1932, a more capacious fuel tank (290 L instead of 182 L) and a simplified oil box were introduced. An engine cooling fan was mounted over the engine in a special shroud. From spring 1932, the exhaust muffler was affixed by three clamps instead of two.

The transmission of the T-26 consisted of single-disk main dry clutch, a gearbox with five gears in the front part of the vehicle, steering clutches, final drives and band brakes. The gearbox was connected to the engine by a drive shaft passing through the vehicle. A gear change lever was mounted directly on the gearbox.

A tank suspension (for each side) consisted of two bogies, four rubber-covered return rollers, a track driving wheel and a track idler. Each bogie consisted of a cast box, four twin rubber-covered road wheels connected by balancing levers and two one-quarter elliptic leaf springs. The cast track driving wheel with removable sprocket ring was located in front, and the track idler with a crank lever tightener was located in the rear part of the vehicle. A track made from chrome-nickel steel was 260 mm (10 in) wide and consisted of 108-109 links.

The T-26 mod. 1931 did not have a radio set. A tank commander communicated with the driver by speaking tube, which was replaced with a signalling lamp in 1932. The T-26 was equipped with one fire extinguisher, a kit of spare parts tools and accessories (including a tank jack), a canvas stowage, and a tow chain fixed on the rear of the hull.

The T-26 could cross 0.75 m high vertical obstacles and 2.1 m wide trenches, ford 0.8 m deep water obstacles, cut 33 cm thick trees and climb 40° gradients. The T-26 proved to be easy to drive.

Beginning in 1937, there was an effort to equip many tanks with a second machine gun in the rear of the turret and an anti-aircraft machine gun on top of it, as well as the addition of two searchlights above the gun for night gunnery, a new VKU-3 command system, and a TPU-3 intercom. Some tanks had vertically stabilised TOP-1 gun telescopic sight. Ammunition stowage for the main gun was improved from 122 rounds to 147. In 1938, the cylindrical turret was replaced with a conical turret, with the same 45 mm model 1934 gun. Some T-26s mod. 1938/1939, equipped with radio set, had a PTK commander's panoramic sight.

Series production

The beginning

The only factory suitable for the T-26 production was the *Bolshevik* Factory in Leningrad, which had experience manufacturing the MS-1 (T-18) light tanks since 1927. It was also planned to use the Stalingrad Tractor Factory which was under construction at that time. But the production of the T-26 proved to be much more complicated than the semi-handicraft assembly of the MS-1, so the planned production of 500 T-26s in 1931 proved to be impossible. The *Bolshevik* Factory needed to convert all tank drawings from inch scale into metric scale, to develop a production technology, special tools and equipment. The first 10 T-26s were assembled in July 1931 – they were identical to British Vickers 6-Ton tanks except for their armament. Soviet tanks were armed with the 37 mm Hotchkiss (PS-1) gun in the right turret and the 7.62 mm DT tank machine gun in the left turret. These T-26s from the development batch were of low quality and made from unarmoured steel, but it was an important test of the new tank production technology.

The series production of the T-26, equipped with new higher turrets with observation window, began in August 1931. Such turrets proved to be more suitable for mass production. The production of the T-26 encountered many problems: a lot of armoured hulls and turrets supplied by the Izhora Factory were of low quality (with cracks) and were 10 mm in thickness instead of the planned 13 mm. Poor production standards were the reason behind the frequent failures of tank engines, gear boxes, springs in suspension, tracks and rubber-covered road wheels of early T-26s. Thirty-five of the 100 T-26s produced by the *Bolshevik* Factory in 1931 had hulls and turrets made from unarmoured steel. Later, it was planned to replace these hulls with armoured ones as well as to mount engines of better quality. Nevertheless, the business plan for 1932 called for 3,000 T-26s (!). For this, the tank workshop of the *Bolshevik* Factory was reorganised into the Factory No. 174 named after K.E. Voroshilov in February 1932. The director of the tank factory became K. Sirken and the chief engineer was S. Ginzburg. But the problems with organizing the complicated new technological processes poor production planning of parts suppliers, a great shortage of qualified engineers and technicians as well as of necessary equipment still resulted in a large percentage of the tanks being flawed, and thus were not accepted by army representatives. On October 26 1932, the Trust of Special Machine Industry consisting of four factories, was established to solve the problem of tank production in the USSR. The planned production of T-26s for 1932 was decreased significantly and special attention was given to increasing the quality of the tanks. A production run of the new model single-turreted T-26 armed with the 45 mm gun was launched in the middle of 1933.

The Factory No. 174 also manufactured a few T-26s for military educational institutions. These were dissected tanks to demonstrate the relative position and function of tank components during training of tankers.

Production in Stalingrad

The prototype of STZ-25 (T-25) wheeled-tracked light tank during tests at the Kubinka Tank Proving Ground. September 1939.

The Stalingrad Tractor Factory (STZ) was considered as one of the factories for production of the T-26 from 1932, but actual production in Stalingrad did not start until August 1933. This process went very slowly, with great difficulties because of delays with deliveries of machining equipment and press tools for the newly built factory. In 1936-1939 the Design Office of the STZ developed several experimental tanks (6 TK, 4 TG, STZ-25, STZ-35) based on the T-26 tank and the STZ-5 transport tractor. For instance, the STZ-25 (T-25) had the turret, rear part of the hull, engine and some transmission details from the T-26 mod. 1938, but the STZ-25 wheeled-tracked tank weighed 11.7 tonnes (12.9 short tons) and had 16-24 mm sloped armour. Factory managers tried to promote tanks of their own design rather than producing T-26s. As a result, the STZ failed to organise the series production of the T-26, but this experience helped to bring the T-34 into production in Stalingrad in 1941. The T-26s produced by STZ had no visual differences from other T-26s, but Stalingrad tanks were less reliable and more expensive.

Modernization and repair

T-26 mod. 1931 (with welded turrets) after repair and modernization. The Military Academy of Mechanization and Motorization named after I. Stalin. 1940.

Some number of early T-26 tanks were repaired in tank units or at factories with the use of later production details. This meant replacing the all-rubber road wheels (except the front wheels) and track idlers with new strengthened ones. In addition, armour was added for the headlight, the armour thickness of the driver's hatch lower door of the twin-turreted tanks was increased from 6 to 10 mm and armoured PT-1 or PTK observation devices were installed. A common hatch above the engine, oil tank, and fuel tank was mounted starting in May 1940. In 1940, 255 T-26s were modernised in this way and in the first half of 1941 another 85 tanks were improved. A central factory responsible for the T-26's repair and modernisation was the Factory of Carrying-and-Conveying Machines named after S. Kirov in Leningrad, and the Factory No. 105 named after L. Kaganovich in Khabarovsk from the beginning of the Great Patriotic War until 1945.

Production in 1941

The Factory No. 174 produced its last T-26 tanks at the beginning of February 1941. After that, the factory began retooling to produce the new and much more complex T-50 light tank. This work was slowed by delays in the delivery of new equipment and series production of the T-50 did not begin on schedule (planned for June 1 1941). As a result, factory management decided to resume the production of the T-26, using T-26 hulls, turrets, and other parts already in stock. About 47 T-26 tanks were assembled and 77 were repaired in July-August 1941 before the factory was relocated from Leningrad to Chelyabinsk in the end of August 1941, and then to Chkalov in the end of September 1941. In addition, the Factory No. 174 produced engines and spare parts for the T-26, installed additional armour plates on some T-26s, replaced flame-throwers with 45 mm tank guns in turrets of 130 KhT-133 flame-throwing tanks, repaired tanks in army units (846 T-26s since the beginning of 1941) and mounted about 75 turrets from the T-26 and the T-50 as bunkers for the defense of Leningrad.

Combat history

The T-26 entered active service for the Red Army (RKKA) in 1932; it was used in many conflicts of 1930s as well as during World War II. The T-26 together with the BT was the main tank of the RKKA during the interwar period.

The T-26 tank first saw action in the Spanish Civil War. The Soviet Union provided Republican Spain with a total of 281 T-26 mod. 1933 tanks starting in October 1936. T-26s were used in almost all military operations of the Spanish Civil War in 1936-1939 and demonstrated there a superiority over the German Panzer I light tanks and Italian CV-33 tankettes armed only with machine guns.

The first military operation of the RKKA in which T-26 light tanks participated was the Soviet-Japanese border conflict, the Battle of Lake Khasan, in July 1938. The 2 Mechanised Brigade, the 32 and the 40 Separate Tank Battalions had 257 T-26s, from which 76 tanks were damaged and 9 burnt towards the end of battle action. A small number of T-26 tanks and flame-throwing tanks based on the T-26 chassis participated in the Battle of Khalkhin Gol in 1939.

On the eve of World War II, T-26s served mainly in separate light tank brigades (each brigade had 256–267 T-26s) and in separate tank battalions of rifle divisions (one company of T-26s consisted of 10-15 tanks). This was the type of tank units that participated in the Soviet invasion of Poland in September 1939 and in the Winter War of December 1939-March 1940. The Winter War proved that the T-26 was obsolete and its design reserve was totally depleted. Finnish anti-tank guns easily penetrated the T-26's thin anti-bullet armour, and tank units equipped with the T-26 suffered significant losses during the breakthrough of the Mannerheim Line in which the flame-throwing tanks based on the T-26 chassis played a significant role.

On June 1 1941 the Red Army had 10,268 T-26 tanks of all models, including armoured combat vehicles based on the T-26 chassis. T-26s composed a majority of the fighting vehicles in Soviet mechanised corps of border military districts. For instance, the Western Special Military District had 1,136 T-26 tanks on June 22 1941 (52% of all tanks in the district). The T-26 (mod. 1938/39, especially) could withstand German tanks (except the Panzer III and Panzer IV) participating in Operation Barbarossa in June 1941. The majority of the Red Army's T-26s were lost in the first months of the German-Soviet War, mainly to enemy artillery and air strikes. Many tanks broke down for technical reasons and lack of spare parts.

Nevertheless, the remaining T-26s participated in combat with the Germans and their allies during the Battle of Moscow in winter 1941-1942, the Battle of Stalingrad and the Battle of the Caucasus in 1942. Some tank units of the Leningrad Front used their T-26 tanks until 1944.

The defeat of the Japanese Kwantung Army in Manchuria in August 1945 was the last military operation in which Soviet T-26s were used.

In the 1930s, T-26 light tanks were delivered to Spain (281), China (82), Turkey (60) and Afghanistan. They were used in the Second Sino-Japanese War by the Chinese in 1938-1944. A considerable number of captured T-26s of different models were used by the Finnish Army during the Continuation War, some tanks served in Finland till 1961. Captured T-26s were also used by the German, Romanian and Hungarian armies.

Twin-turreted tanks

- **T-26 model 1931** — twin-turreted version armed with two DT tank machine guns. The first series-produced variant of the T-26 which was equipped with turrets differing from the initial Vickers design (Soviet turrets were higher and had an observation window). Tanks produced from 1931 to March 1932 had a riveted hull and turrets, a muffler affixed with two clamps, and lacked any cover over the air outlet window. About 1,177 T-26 mod. 1931 tanks armed with machine guns were accepted by the Red Army, which had 1,015 such twin-turreted tanks on April 1 1933.
- **T-26 model 1931 with gun plus machine gun armament** — twin-turreted version with a 37 mm gun in the right turret (some modern sources mention this tank as **T-26 model 1932**). There were two models of 37 mm guns in the USSR suitable for mounting in light tanks that time - the Hotchkiss gun (or its Soviet improved variant PS-1), and the more powerful PS-2 gun developed by P. Syachentov. The latter was superior, but only experimental models existed. Therefore, the first 10 pre-production T-26s, which had a design identical to the Vickers 6-Ton, were equipped with a Hotchkiss gun in the right turret to increase firepower compared to the machine gun armed Vickers tank. The experimental PS-2 gun was mounted on only three T-26 tanks, the right turrets of which were replaced with small gun turrets from the T-35-1 (prototype of the T-35 heavy tank).

Twin-turreted T-26 mod. 1931 with riveted hull and turrets, armed with the 37 mm Hotchkiss gun (PS-1) in the right turret. Battle of Tolvajärvi. December 1939.

As the series production of the PS-2 gun was delayed, the Main Artillery Agency of the RKKA gave preference to a new gun. It was developed by the Artillery Design Office of the *Bolshevik* Factory, constructed from parts taken from the previously purchased German 37 mm anti-tank gun developed by Rheinmetall and the PS-2 gun. This system was successfully tested and the Artillery Factory No. 8 named after M. Kalinin started its series production under the designator B-3 (5K). The B-3 gun had less recoil and a smaller breech compared to the PS-2, so it could be easily mounted in the normal machine gun turret of the T-26. The first twin-turreted T-26 was armed with a B-3 gun in the right turret in autumn 1931. Unfortunately, series production of the B-3 gun proceeded slowly due to poor production standards (none of 225 guns produced in 1931 were accepted by army representatives; it took until 1933 to complete the original order for 300 guns placed in August of 1931). In addition, completed B-3 guns would be mounted on BT-2 light tanks after summer 1932. This meant that twin-turreted T-26 tanks would continue to be equipped with old 37 mm Hotchkiss (PS-1) guns. As production of the PS-1 gun had ended, some guns were taken from military supply depots and scrapped MS-1(T-18) tanks.

The initial plan was to arm every fifth T-26 with the 37 mm gun in the right turret, but the final proportion was somewhat higher. About 450 twin-turreted T-26 mod. 1931 tanks mounting the 37 mm gun in the right turret were produced in 1931–1933 (including only 20-30 tanks with the B-3 gun). There were 392 T-26 mod. 1931 tanks with gun plus machine gun armament in the Red Army on 1 April 1933.

Twin-turreted T-26 armed with the 76.2 mm recoilless gun designed by L. V. Kurchevsky in the right turret. 1934.

Twin-turreted T-26 (with the 37 mm Hotchkiss gun (PS-1) in the right turret), equipped with the radio station No. 7N and the hand-rail frame antenna on the hull. Military exercises. 1934.

- **T-26 (BPK)** (BPK stands for *batal'onnaya pushka Kurchevskogo* or "battalion gun by Kurchevsky") - twin-turreted version with a 76.2 mm recoilless gun (or "dynamic reaction gun", as it was called at the time) in the right turret. At the end of 1933 M. Tukhachevsky suggested equipping some T-26 mod. 1931 tanks with the 76.2 mm BPK recoilless gun designed by L.V. Kurchevsky in a right turret to increase a fire power. One prototype tank was built in 1934. BPK had a muzzle velocity of 500 m/s (1,640 ft/s) and a range of 4 km (2.5 mi). The tank was able to carry 62 4-kg rounds. The test performed on 9 March 1934 demonstrated a significant increase in firepower, but the recoilless gun proved difficult to reload on the move and the powerful jet blast projected behind the weapon when fired would be dangerous to infantrymen behind the tank. Shortcomings were also observed in the design of the gun itself, and so the planned rearmament of twin-turreted T-26 tanks with recoilless guns did not take place.

- **T-26TU** (TU stands for *tank upravleniya* or "command tank") - twin-turreted version with a simplex radio station No. 7N (communication range - 10 km) and a hand-rail frame antenna on the hull. The antenna lead was located in the front part of the underturret box roof between the turrets. The vehicle was intended for platoon (and higher) commanders. Three such tanks were successfully tested in September 1932 and seven more radio stations were delivered to the Factory No. 174, but it is unknown whether they were ever mounted on twin-turreted T-26 tanks. Series production of twin-turreted command radio tanks was scheduled to begin on January 1 1933, but this did not occur because radio stations No. 7N were in short supply and because of the introduction of single-turreted T-26s with series-produced 71-TK-1 radio stations.

Additionally, one twin-turreted T-26 was given to the Research Institute of Communication in March 1932 to develop special tank communication devices. The plan was to equip each tank with a keyphone, while a platoon commander's tank would be equipped with a telephone switch for 6 subscribers (four for the tanks in the platoon, one for communication with infantry and one for contacting headquarters). A special terminal block was mounted on the rear of the tank so that communication wires could be connected. The work remained experimental.

Single-turreted tanks

- **T-26 model 1933** — single turret version armed with 45 mm 20K tank gun and DT tank machine gun. This version had a new cylindrical turret with a large rear niche. Some tanks were equipped with a 71-TK-1 radio station with a hand-rail antenna around the turret (so-called radio tanks). They were upgraded in 1935 with a welded hull and turret, and again in 1936 with a rear DT tank machine gun in the turret. In 1937, some tanks were equipped with an anti-aircraft machine gun and a searchlight. The model 1933 was the most numerous variant.

- **T-26 model 1938** — new conical turret, small changes in hull parts, increased volume of fuel tanks. Tank gun mod. 1937 and mod. 1938 were equipped with an electric breechblock and a vertically stabilized TOP-1 telescopic sight (or a TOS telescopic sight on the 1938 model).

- **T-26 model 1939 (T-26-1)** — underturret box with sloped armoured plates, rear machine gun removed on some tanks, 97 hp engine. Tanks built after 1940 were equipped with an underturret box made from 20 mm homogeneous armour, a unified observation device, and a new turret ring. Some tanks were equipped with armoured screens. About 1,975 T-26 tanks with a conical turret (T-26 mod. 1938, T-26 mod. 1939) were produced.

T-26 mod. 1933 with applique armour after running trials. Spring 1940.

- **T-26 screened** - tank with additional armour plating (applique armour). Some modern sources mention this tank as **T-26E** (E stands for *ekranirovanny* or "screened"). The Factory No. 174 developed the design of 30-40 mm applique armour for all types of single-turreted T-26s during the Winter War. On December 30, 1939, factory tests proved that the T-26 with applique armour successfully resisted fire from a 45 mm anti-tank gun at a range from 400-500 m. Side and front armoured plates were mounted with the use of blunt bolts and electric welding. Toward the middle of February 1940, the RKKA received 27 screened T-26 mod. 1939 tanks and 27 KhT-133 flame-throwing tanks; an additional 15 T-26 mod. 1939 tanks were armoured by workshops of the 8 Army in Suoyarvi in the beginning of March 1940. All in all, 69 T-26s with applique armour were used during the Winter War and 20 more were delivered to tank units after the end of the war. Combat use proved that Finnish light anti-tank guns could not penetrate the armour of these tanks.

The T-26 mod. 1939 with applique armour weighed 12 tonnes (13 short tons), which caused an overload of the chassis, transmission, and engine of the light tank. Drivers were advised to use low gears only.

During the Great Patriotic War, a mounting of 15-40 mm applique armour on about a hundred different T-26s was performed by local factories in Leningrad in 1941-1942, during the Siege of Odessa (1941), the Battle for Moscow and the Siege of Sevastopol (1941–1942). A cutting of armoured plates was more rough than developed during the Winter War; the majority of these modified tanks did not have a moving armoured gun mask as seen in Factory No. 174's original design, and some tanks had front applique armour only.

Artillery tanks

T-26 mod. 1931 with the A-43 welded turret developed by N. Dyrenkov. Note the ball mount for the DT tank machine gun. Leningrad. 1933.

- **T-26 with the A-43 turret** - artillery T-26 or "tank of fire support" with a turret developed by self-taught inventor N. Dyrenkov at the Experimental Design Office of the Department of Mechanization and Motorization of the RKKA (UMM RKKA). Two types of turrets, armed with the 76 mm regimental gun mod. 1927 and DT tank machine gun in a ball mount, were assembled by the Izhora Factory. They were partially pressed and welded. The first variety was installed on the T-26 mod. 1931 in February 1932 and the second type was used in November 1932 (in the last case, the rear armoured plate of underturret box was made sloping).

It was found that the A-43 turret was very tight for two crewmembers; it had insufficient observation field; there was not any turret ventilation which made continuous gunfire difficult; and it was hard to rotate the turret manually. At the beginning of 1933, a new 76 mm KT tank gun mod. 1927/32 with reduced (from 900 mm to 500 mm) recoil length was installed into the A-43 turret. Nevertheless, it was proved again that the turret was still a very tight place for crew members. In addition, the ammunition stowage for 54 rounds was unsuccessful. As a result, the military refused the A-43 turret.

- **T-26-4** — artillery tank with enlarged turret armed with the 76.2 mm KT tank gun mod. 1927/32 (some modern sources mention this tank as **T-26A**, A stands for *artil'eriysky* or "artillery"). The turret was developed by the *Bolshevik* Factory (since February 1932 - by the Design Office of the established Factory No. 174) in 1931-1932; it was installed on the T-26 mod. 1931 in November 1932. Unlike the A-43 turret, the turret by Factory No. 174 was much more convenient for the crew. The turret of the T-26-4 was quite similar to main turret of the T-28 medium tank.

The T-26-4 with the KT tank gun passed tests successfully and five vehicles were built in 1933-1934 as pilot batch. Initially it was planned to arm three of these T-26-4 with the 76.2 mm KT tank gun mod. 1927/32 and the other two tanks with the 76.2 mm PS-3 tank gun. The PS-3 tank gun was developed at the Experimental Engineering-Mechanical Department (OKMO) of the Factory No. 174 by engineer P. Syachentov. The PS-3 had better specifications in comparison with the series-produced KT tank gun and also had several technical innovations (foot firing switch, original training gear, travelling position fixing, binocular optical sight). The T-26-4 armed with the PS-3 tank gun was tested in October 1933 but it was found that the PS-3 was too powerful for the T-26 light tank - turret's race ring and hull roof were deformed during gun fire, and the suspension springs were damaged. It was decided to arm the T-26-4 with the 76.2 mm KT tank gun only. All five experimental T-26-4 artillery tanks were tested during military exercises near Leningrad in September 1934 before scheduled series production of 50 such vehicles in 1935. But on September 19, 1934 an incident with a T-26-4 took place: a blow-back because of shell case destruction during gun fire. Despite the fact that this defect was unrelated to turret design, the military representatives cancelled the order to produce the T-26-4. Also the work to design turretless AT-1 artillery tanks armed with the powerful 76.2 mm PS-3 tank gun started at that time. Nevertheless, the T-26-4's turret construction was the design used in the series-produced BT-7A artillery tank.

In 1939, the Armored Directorate of the Red Army (ABTU RKKA) ordered the development of a new conical turret for the T-26 similar to the BT-7's turret and to arm it with the 76.2 mm L-10 tank gun. But engineers of the Factory No. 174 felt it was impossible to implement this project because it would lead to a significant overload of T-26's chassis.

Armoured combat vehicles

A large variety of different armoured combat vehicles were developed on the T-26 chassis in the 1930s. Among them were KhT-26, KhT-130 and KhT-133 flame tanks (552, 401 and 269 vehicles were produced, respectively); T-26T artillery tractors (197 were produced); TT-26 and TU-26 radio-controlled tanks (162 radio-controlled tanks of all models were produced); ST-26 bridge-laying tanks (71 were produced); SU-5 self-propelled guns (33 were produced); experimental armoured cargo/personnel carriers, reconnaissance vehicles, and many others. Various vehicle-mounted equipment was developed for the T-26, including tank mine sweeps, inflatable pontoons and a snorkel for fording water obstacles.

Foreign Variants
- **7.5 cm Pak 97/38(f) auf Pz.740(r)** - Ten Pak 97-38 anti-tank guns with shields were experimentally mounted on captured Soviet T-26 light tank chassis, resulting in vehicles designated 7.5 cm Pak 97/38(f) auf Pz.740(r). These self-propelled guns served with the 3 Company of the 563 Anti-Tank Battalion before being replaced by Marder III on 1 March 1944.

Survivors

There are about 45 T-26 tanks of various models preserved in different museums and military schools (mainly Russian, Spanish and Finnish). The most notable of them are:

T-26 mod. 1931 with riveted hull and turrets. Central Museum of the Great Patriotic War in Moscow, Russia. 2008.

- Twin-turreted T-26 mod. 1931 in the Central Museum of the Great Patriotic War in Moscow (Russia) - this tank from the 115 Rifle Division with shell holes was raised from a river bottom on the site of river crossing at Nevsky Pyatachok in July 1989 by *Katran* diving club. The vehicle was restored at the Pärnu Training Tank Regiment of the Leningrad Military District. It was donated to the museum in February 1998. Only two such vehicles are preserved at the present time.
- Twin-turreted T-26 mod. 1931 with gun plus machine gun armament and riveted hull in the Kubinka Tank Museum in Moscow Oblast (Russia). The single surviving twin-turreted T-26 armed with the 37 mm gun.
- T-26 mod. 1933 in the Central Armed Forces Museum in Moscow (Russia) - this late production variant was transferred from Kubinka Tank Museum in 1980s.
- T-26 mod. 1933 in the Museum-Diorama "Breaching of the Blockade of the Leningrad" in Mar'ino village near Kirovsk, Leningrad Oblast (Russia) - this tank with a large shell hole on the right side of the hull and without turret was raised from a river bottom at Nevsky Pyatachok in May 2003.
- T-26 mod. 1933 in the Museum of the Northwestern Front in Staraya Russa, Novgorod Oblast (Russia) - this tank was raised from the Lovat River in 1981 and became a monument to Soviet tankers in Korovitchino village (Novgorod Oblast). The vehicle was given to the museum in May 2004. The tank has inauthentic tracks.

T-26 mod. 1933. El Goloso Museum in Madrid, Spain. 2007.

- T-26 mod. 1933 in the El Goloso Baracks Museum in Madrid (Spain) - the tank (Spanish tactical number 135) with Nationalist Spanish markings with pressed gun mask is armed with a Hotchkiss machine gun instead of a DT tank machine gun. Produced in 1936. The anti-aircraft machine gun and the hand-rail radio antenna are late dummies.

T-26 mod. 1933. Parola Tank Museum, Finland. 2006.

- T-26 mod. 1933 in the Parola Tank Museum (Finland) - Finnish tactical number Ps 163-33, in drivable condition.
- T-26 mod. 1933 in the Parola Tank Museum (Finland) - this tank is described in many sources as early version of the T-26 mod. 1933. But in reality this is the Finnish war-time modernization (Finnish tactical number Ps 163-16) of a hull from KhT-26 flame-throwing tank (which

can be identified by rivets for mounting of a burning mixture tank, rivets for hinges of a filling hatch on the left side and a welded drain port on the right side behind a front track bogie) with a mounted riveted turret with a small rear niche from the early BT-5 light tank.

- T-26 mod. 1933 in the Parola Tank Museum (Finland) - the Finnish wartime modernization (Finnish tactical number Ps 163-28) of a hull from KhT-26 flame-throwing tank with a mounted turret from the BT-7 light tank.
- T-26 mod. 1939 in the Kubinka Tank Museum, Moscow Oblast (Russia) - this tank with pressed gun mask is in drivable condition (the GAZ-41 engine from the BRDM-2 was installed in 2005). The tank has combat damage taken during the Great Patriotic War (many marks from armour-piercing bullets and a welded hole on the right side of the turret from a 50 mm shell).
- T-26 mod. 1939 in the Parola Tank Museum, (Finland) - the Finnish war-time modernization (Finnish tactical number Ps 164-7); a hull from a KhT-133 flame-throwing tank with a mounted turret from the T-26 mod. 1938/1939 and a ball mount for the DT tank machine gun in a hull front armoured plate.
- KhT-130 flame-throwing tank in the Kubinka Tank Museum, Moscow Oblast (Russia) - in reality this is the TU-26 teletank control vehicle with a dummy flame-thrower.
- KhT-130 flame-throwing tank in the Military Unit No. 05776 in Borzya, Chita Oblast (Russia) - monument (since 1995) with an incomplete chassis (one track bogie is missing; tracks and driving wheels were taken from the M3 Stuart American light tank. Before 1990 the vehicle stood in the territory of one of military units of the Soviet 39 Army (located in Mongolia) of the Transbaikal Military District. The single preserved KhT-130 at the present time.

Source (edited): "http://en.wikipedia.org/wiki/T-26"

T-28

The Soviet **T-28** was among the world's first medium tanks. The prototype was completed in 1931 and production began in late 1932. It was an infantry-support tank intended to break through fortified defences. The T-28 was designed to complement the heavier T-35, with which it shared many components. The type would not have that much success in combat, but it played an important role as a development project for the Soviet designers. A series of new ideas and solutions were tried out on the T-28 and were later incorporated in future models.

Design history

Production of the T-28

The T-28 was in many ways similar to the British Vickers A1E1 Independent tank. This tank greatly influenced tank design in the period between the wars, although only one prototype was manufactured in 1926. The Kirov Factory in Leningrad began manufacturing a tank, which was based on the British Independent in 1932. The T-28 tank was officially approved on August 11, 1933. The T-28 had one large turret with a 76.2mm gun and two smaller turrets with 7.62mm machine guns. A total of 503 T-28 tanks were manufactured over a period of 8 years from 1933 to 1941.

Combat history

T-28s in combat in 1941, Note the anti-aircraft machinegun mount on the turret top.

The T-28 was deployed during the Invasion of Poland and the Winter War against Finland. During the initial stages of the Winter War, the tank was used in direct fire missions against Finnish pillboxes. In the course of these operations it was found that the armour was inadequate and programs were initiated to upgrade it. Frontal plates were upgraded from 50 mm to 80 mm and side and rear plates to 40 mm thickness. With this up-armoured version the Red Army broke through the main Finnish defensive fortification, the Mannerheim Line

According to Russian historian M. Kolomietz's book *T-28. Three-headed Stalin's Monster*, over 200 T-28s were knocked out during the Winter War, but only 20 of them were in irrecoverable losses (including 2 captured by the Finnish Army). Due to proximity of the Kirov Plant, all other knocked-out tanks were repaired, some of them over five times.

T-28 tanks, with horseshoe radio antennas

The Finns knew the T-28 as the *Postivaunu* ("mail wagon" or stagecoach), a name which alluded to Finnish troops' discovery of Red Army field mail sacks inside the first destroyed T-28. Another explanation is that the high profile of the tank resembled the old west stagecoaches of the United States. Finns captured two T-28s during the Winter War and five in Continuation War, for a total of 7 vehicles.

The Soviets had 411 T-28 tanks when the Germans invaded the Soviet Union in June 1941. Most T-28s were lost during the first two months of the invasion, many of them abandoned after mechanical breakdown. Some T-28s took part in the 1941 winter defence of Leningrad and Moscow, but after late 1941, they were rare in Red Army service; a few were operated by enemy forces.

Today three T-28s remain, two in Finland and one in Moscow. One restored T-28 is on display in Finnish field camouflage in the Parola Tank Museum, Finland.

Assessment

Although the T-28 was rightly considered ineffective by 1941, it is worth remembering that when the Red Army was fielding the first T-28s in 1933, the French Army was still largely equipped with the FT-17, and the Reichswehr had no tanks at all. No army had a series-production medium tank comparable to the T-28 for several years.

The T-28 had a number of advanced features for the time, including radio (in all tanks) and anti-aircraft machine-gun mounts. Just before the Second World War, many received armor upgrades, bringing its protection on par with the early *PzKpfw* IV, although its suspension and layout were outdated.

The T-28 had significant flaws. The plunger-spring type suspension was poor, but many of the better suspension designs used in World War II tanks had not yet been developed. The engine and transmission were troublesome. Worst of all, the design was not flexible. Although the T-28 and early *PzKpfw* IV were comparable in armour and firepower, the sound basic design of the *PzKpfw* IV allowed it to be significantly upgraded, while the T-28 was a poor basis for improvement.

Unfortunately for the Red Army, by the time the T-28 saw combat in 1939, events had overtaken it. The 1930s saw the development of the first reliable high-speed suspensions, the first purpose-designed antitank guns, and a gradual increase in the firepower of tanks. The Spanish Civil War showed that infantry units with small, towed anti-tank guns could defeat most contemporary tanks, and made the under-armoured tanks from the early 1930s particularly vulnerable.

Despite heavy losses, in the Winter War the Red Army's 20th Tank Brigade, equipped with T-28s, fulfilled its mission to break the defensive Mannerheim Line. As an infantry-support tank, designed to support infantry in breakthrough operations, the T-28 in general was successful for an early 1930s design.

Variants

- **T-28 Model 1934** or **T-28A**—main production model with the same machinegun turrets, and similar main turret as the T-35 heavy tank and Model 27/32 76.2mm gun.
- **T-28 Model 1938** or **T-28B**—version with improved L-10 76.2 mm gun (from 16.5 calibres to 26 calibres), improved gun stabilization system and improved Model M-17L engine.
- **T-28E** or **T-28C** — 1940 addition of appliqué armour in response to poor performance in Finland. Total front armour was increased to 80 mm, weight to 32 t, and road speed dropped to 23 km/h
- **T-28 Model 1940** — the final batch of about twelve tanks had the same conical turret as late-production T-35 tanks.

Experimental models

Several self-propelled guns, the IT-28 bridging tank, and an engineering vehicle with mine rollers were tested on the T-28 tank chassis, but none was accepted for production. The T-29 was a prototype medium tank, a modernized T-28 with Christie suspension — a later version of this vehicle was considered for the competition of prototypes which led to the T-34, but by then it was outdated (not to be confused with a Grotte tank project also called T-29). The T-28 also served as a testbed for the KV tank suspension.

Operators

- Soviet Union
- Finland – captured seven Soviet T-28 tanks during the Winter War and the Continuation War.
- Hungary – the Hungarian Army used one captured T-28 tank in the summer of 1941.
- Nazi Germany – Germany captured and made operational at least one T-28 during Operation Barbarossa, designated Panzerkampfwagen T-28 746(r).
- Turkey – According to one source, two were sold to Turkey in 1935, along with 60 T-26, five T-27 tankettes, and about 60 BA-6 armoured cars to form the 1st Tank Regiment of the 2nd Cavalry Division at Luleburgaz.
- Spain – Also according to some sources, a single T-28 was sent as aid to the Republic in the Spanish Civil War during 1936–39, but its combat record is unknown.

Source (edited): "http://en.wikipedia.org/wiki/T-28"

T-35

The **T-35** was a Soviet multi-turreted heavy tank of the interwar period and early Second World War that saw limited production and service with the Red Army. It was the only five-turreted heavy tank in the world to reach production but proved to be slow and mechanically unreliable. Most of the T-35 tanks still operational at the time of Operation

Barbarossa were lost due to mechanical failure rather than enemy action.

Outwardly it was large but internally the spaces were cramped with the fighting compartments separated from each other. Some of the turrets obscured the entrance hatches.

Production history

The T-35 was developed by the OKMO design bureau of the Bolshevik Factory, which began work on a heavy tank in 1930. Two teams developed separate designs. The team headed by German engineer Grotte worked on the 100-ton four-turreted TG-5 tank, armed with a 107 mm naval gun, using pneumatic servo-controls and pneumatic suspension. This project was later cancelled.

The concept of large, multi-turreted breakthrough tanks was favoured by several European armies in the 1920s and 1930s. Designs existed in Britain, France, and Germany for such vehicles. The second OKMO team, headed by N. Tsiets, worked on a tank inspired by the British Vickers A1E1 Independent.

By July 1932, a prototype of a 35 ton tank with a 76.2 mm tank gun was completed. The first prototype was further enhanced with four smaller turrets, two with 37 mm guns and two with machine guns. This first prototype had severe defects in its transmission and was considered too complex and expensive for mass production. Therefore work on it was stopped and a new simpler prototype was built.

This new prototype received a new engine, new gearbox and improved transmission. The decision was also made to standardise the turrets used on the T-35 with those used on the T-28, a triple-turreted medium tank. The small machine-gun turrets were identical on the two tanks. The large main turret housing the 76.2 mm gun was nearly identical, but those used on the T-28 had an additional, rear-firing machine gun.

On August 11, 1933, the T-35 was accepted for production. Engineering was shifted to the Kharkov Locomotive Factory, and two batches of ten vehicles were completed.

The experiences gained with the two prototypes were used for the main production T-35 Model 1935, which was again improved from the second prototype, with a longer chassis, improved hull and 45-mm guns in place of the 37's. It started production in 1935, and about 35 were built by 1938. In general, throughout its production run small improvements were made to the individual tanks. Production tanks had turrets similar to the ones on the BT-5, but without the rear overhang. Some examples had flamethrowers instead of one of the 45 mm guns. The final batch was a run of six T-35 model 1938s, which had new turrets with sloped armour all around, as well as modified side skirts and new idler wheels.

Western and Russian historians disagree about the inspiration for the T-35's design. The former argue it was inspired by the British Vickers A1E1 Independent tank, but this is rejected by many Russian specialists. It is impossible to know the truth, but there is strong evidence to support Western claims, not least failed Soviet attempts to purchase the A1E1. At the same time, the influence of German engineers developing similar designs in the late 1920s at their Kama base in the Soviet Union cannot be discounted. What is clear is that borrowing military technology and ideas from other nations was common to the majority of the armed forces in the inter-war years. The Red Army, with its purchase of the British Vickers Carden Loyd tankette, Vickers E-Light and Cruiser Mk II Medium tanks, and the American Christie suspension, was clearly one of the leading exponents of this practice.

Due to its high cost, the production run of the T-35 ended at just sixty-one tanks.

Combat history

The T-35 served with the 5th Separate Heavy Tank Brigade in Moscow, primarily for parade duties, from 1935 until 1940. In June 1940, the question was raised whether to withdraw the T-35s from frontline service, with the option to either convert them to heavy self propelled artillery, or to assign them to the various military academies. The choice was made to use them up in combat instead and the surviving vehicles were collected together into the 67th and 68th Tank Regiments of the 34th Tank Division, which served with the 8th Mechanized Corps in the Kiev Special Military District.

During Operation Barbarossa, ninety percent of the T-35s lost by the 67th and 68th Tank Regiments were lost not to enemy action but through either mechanical failure or because they were abandoned and destroyed by their crews. The most common causes of breakdown were transmission-related. The last recorded action of the T-35 took place during the early stages of the Battle of Moscow. Four machines were used in training facilities in the Soviet rear. One of these still exists and is accessible to visitors at the Kubinka Tank Museum near Moscow.

The T-35 is sometimes cited as having participated in the Winter War against Finland, but according to Soviet sources it did not. In fact, a prototype (multi-turreted) SMK tank had been sent to the front for testing. This tank was disabled by a Finnish land mine and all attempts to recover the 55-ton behemoth failed. Finnish photographs of the previously unknown tank were mistakenly designated *T-35C* by German intelligence.

Variants

- T-35-1: Prototype
- T-35-2: Prototype
- T-35A: Production model.
- T-35B: New engine. Only the prototype was produced.
- SU-7: Prototypes with a 254 mm gun, 305 mm howitzer, and 400 mm mortar. Weighed over 106 tons.

See also

- Char 2C: tank with similar design
- List of tanks
- List of Soviet tanks
- Vickers A1E1 Independent: Almost completely identical

References

- Zaloga, Steven J.; James Grandsen

Type 95 Heavy Tank

The **Type 95 Heavy Tank** was the final version of the Japanese multi-turreted designs in commission during the time periods of World War I and World War II. Modeled from Axis German and Italian tank designs, this tank featured 2 turrets, the main armament being a 70mm cannon, and its secondary turret mounting a 37mm gun and two 6.5mm machine guns. Only the prototype was ever produced, in 1934.

Source (edited): "http://en.wikipedia.org/wiki/Type_95_Heavy_Tank"

Vickers 6-Ton

The **Vickers 6-Ton Tank** or **Vickers Mark E** was a British light tank designed as a private project at Vickers. It was not purchased by the British Army, but was picked up by a large number of foreign armed forces and was copied almost exactly by the Soviets as the T-26. It was also the direct predecessor of the Polish 7TP tank. By the start of World War II it was the second most common tank design in the world after the Renault FT-17.

History

The first Mark E was built in 1928 by a design team that included the famed tank designers John Valentine Carden and Vivian Loyd. The hull was made of riveted steel plates, 1 inch (25 mm) thick at the front and over most of the turrets, and about 3/4 inch (19 mm) thick on the rear of the hull. The power was provided by an Armstrong Siddeley Puma engine of 80–95 horsepower (60–70 kW) (depending on the version), which gave it a top speed of 22 mph (35 km/h) on roads.

The suspension used two axles, each of which carried a two-wheel bogie to which a second set of bogies was connected with a leaf spring. Upward movement of either set of bogies would force the other down through the spring. This was considered to be a fairly good system and offered better than normal cross-country performance although it could not compare with the contemporary Christie suspension. High strength steel tracks gave over 3000 miles (5000 km) of life which was considerably better than most designs of the era.

The tank was built in two versions:
- **Type A** with two turrets, each mounting a Vickers machine gun.
- **Type B** with a single two-man turret mounting a single machine gun and a short-barrelled 47 mm cannon.

The Type B proved to be a real innovation, it was found that the two-man turret dramatically increased the rate of fire of either weapon, while still allowing both to be fired at the same time. This design, which they referred to as a *duplex mounting*, became common on almost all tanks designed after the Mark E.

The British Army evaluated the Mark E, but rejected it, apparently due to questions about the reliability of the suspension. Vickers then started advertising the design to all buyers, and soon received a trickle of orders eventually including USSR, Greece, Poland, Bolivia, Siam, Finland, Portugal, China and Bulgaria. A Thai order was placed, but taken over by the British when the war started. Vickers built a total of 153 (the most common figure) Mark E's.

Experience with the Polish machines showed that the engine tended to overheat due to poor airflow over the air-cooled Puma engine. This was addressed by the addition of large air vents on either side of the hull. For a new Belgian order the design was modified to use the Rolls-Royce Phantom II water-cooled engine instead. This engine would not fit in the rear, and had to be mounted along the left side of the tank, requiring the turret to be moved to the right and rearward. One example of the resulting **Mark F** was tested by Belgium, but rejected. Nevertheless the new hull was used, with the older engine, in the sales to Finland and Siam.

The Mark E was also developed as a cargo vehicle, and purchased by the British Army in small numbers as artillery tractors to haul their large 60 pounder (127 mm) artillery guns. Twelve were ordered by the Army as the *Dragon, Medium Mark IV'*, while China purchased 23 and India 18.

Poland was generally happy with the design, and purchased 50 and licensed it for local production. Modifying it with larger air intakes, their own machine gun, 360-degree Gundlach periscope. and a Diesel engine, the design entered service as the 7TP. Only the original 38 entered service, 12 remained unassembled and later used for spares. Out of 38 original two-turreted tanks, 22 were later converted to single turret version with a modified turret and the 47 mm main gun (Type B standard).

The Soviets were also happy with the design and licensed it for production.

However in their case local production started as the T-26, and eventually over 12,000 were built in various versions. The Soviet early twin-turret T-26s had 7.62 mm DT machine guns in each turret, or a mix of one machine gun turret and one 37 mm gun turret. Later, more common versions mounted a 45 mm gun and two DT machine guns. The final versions of the T-26 had welded construction and, eventually, sloped armor on the hull and turret. Because the T-26 was in such wide use and was a reliable platform, a variety of engineer vehicles were built on the chassis, including flamethrowers and bridgelayers. A novel radio-controlled demolition tank was built on the T-26 chassis also. During the Spanish Civil War the Soviet Union sent the T-26 to the Republican Army. The Italians, after suffering losses from Republican's T-26 during the battle of Guadalajara (1937), captured some of these tanks which served as a model for their M11/39 and M13/40 light/medium tanks.

Polish Vickers E in 1938

In 1939, during the Soviet-Finnish Winter War, the Finnish armoured forces consisted of around thirty-two obsolete Renault FT-17 tanks, some Vickers-Carden-Lloyd Mk. IVs and Model 33s, which were equipped with machine guns, and 26 Vickers Armstrongs 6-ton tanks. The latter had been re-equipped with 37 mm Bofors AT-guns after the outbreak of the war. Only 13 of these tanks managed to get to the front in time to participate in the battles. At the Battle of Honkaniemi on February 26, 1940, the Finns employed their Vickers tanks for the first - and only - time against Russian armour during the Winter War. The results were disastrous. Of the thirteen available Finnish Vickers 6-ton tanks only six were in fighting condition and able to participate in the first assault on the Soviet lines - to make matters worse, one of the tanks was forced to stop, unable to cross a wide trench. The remaining five continued onwards a few hundred meters but ran into dozens of Soviet tanks in the village of Honkaniemi. The Finnish tanks managed to knock out three Soviet tanks but were soon themselves knocked-out. In the skirmishes that followed, the Finns lost two more Vickers tanks.

In 1941, the Finns rearmed their Vickers 6-Ton tanks with the Soviet 45 mm gun and re-designated them as **T-26E**. These tanks were used by the Finnish Army during the Continuation War. 19 rebuilt Vickers tanks, along with 75 T-26s continued in Finnish service after the end of the Second World War. Some of these tanks were kept as training tanks until 1959, when they were finally phased out and replaced by newer British and Soviet tanks.

Operators

- Bolivia - used one twin-turret tank Type A and two single-turret tanks Type B. The Bolivian Vickers tanks were the first to see combat service, also the first tanks to see combat in the Americas - in 1933 they were used in the Chaco War against Paraguay. All of them were destroyed or captured by Paraguayan forces. See Tank warfare in the Chaco War.
- Bulgaria - bought 8 single-turret Mk.E Type B tanks, used for training only.
- Republic of China - used 20 single-turret tanks Vickers Mk.E Type B. They were used in combat against the Japanese in Shanghai in 1937.
- Finland - used 33 tanks since 1938. They were armed initially with a short-barreled 47 mm gun and later hastily equipped with a 37 mm Bofors anti-tank gun as their main gun. They were used in the Winter War with the USSR. After this war, the Finns rearmed Mark E tanks with captured Soviet long 45 mm guns as used in the T-26. The Finns designated the rebuilt Vickers tanks as: **T-26E**. They were used in combat from 1941–44 and remained in service as training tanks until 1959.
- Greece - 2 type A and 2 type B for tests, acquired during or prior to 1935.
- Paraguay - One double-turret Vickers Mk.E Type A tank captured to Bolivia, later used as monument, returned to Bolivia in 1994.
- Poland - used 38 tanks since 1932: 22 Type B and 16 Type A tanks. Polish tanks had large air intakes behind the crew compartment as a significant feature. Poland also bought a license and developed an own improved model 7TP. Vickers Mk.E (Vickers E) tanks fought in the Invasion of Poland.

Finnish Vickers

- Portugal - 2 tanks for tests
- Soviet Union - the first buyer of Vickers Mk.E tanks. In 1931 bought 15 twin-turret tanks Mk.E Type A, and a license. The Soviets next started building and developing own improved tanks T-26 (about 12 000 made).
- Spain - one ex-Bolivian single-turret Vickers Mk.E Type B tank bought from Paraguay, and a

number of Soviet-made T-26.
- Thailand (formerly Siam) - used 30 Vickers Mk.E Type B, which saw combat during the French-Thai War in French Indochina.
- United Kingdom - used only 4 tanks for training.

Source (edited): "http://en.wikipedia.org/wiki/Vickers_6-Ton"

Vickers A1E1 Independent

The **Independent A1E1** was a multi-turreted tank designed by the British armaments manufacturer Vickers during the interwar period. Although it only ever reached the prototype stage it influenced many other tank designs.

The A1E1 design can be seen as a possible influence on the Soviet T-100 and T-28 tanks, the German *Neubaufahrzeug* tanks, and the British Medium Mk III and Cruiser Mk I (triple turret) tank designs. The Soviet T-35 tank was based extremely closely on its plans and layout.

Design

The Independent was a multi-turret design, having a central gun turret armed with the 3 pounder (47 mm) gun, and four subsidiary turrets each armed with a 0.303 inch Vickers machine gun. The subsidiary turrets were mounted two at the front and two at the rear, the turrets at the corners being able to elevate to engage aircraft. The tank was designed to have heavy firepower, self-defence capability, and superiority to enemy weapons. It had a crew of eight men, the commander communicating with the crew through an intercom system. The Independent was never used in combat, but many other armies *copied* it.

History

A1E1 at Bovington

In 1924 the General Staff of the British Army ordered the prototype of a heavy tank, which became known as the Independent. Largely designed by Walter Gordon Wilson, its 35.8 litre V12 air cooled engine was designed by Armstrong Siddeley, and it also incorporated a new hydraulic braking system which had to be specially developed due to its weight and speed. The prototype was delivered to the War Office in 1926, but was abandoned due to a lack of funds.

The tank was the subject of industrial and political espionage, the plans ending up in the Soviet Union, where they may have influenced the design of the T-28 and T-35 tanks.

The Independent is preserved at the Bovington Tank Museum in the UK.
Source (edited): "http://en.wikipedia.org/wiki/Vickers_A1E1_Independent"

AMERICAN ROCKABILLY GUITARISTS

Table of Contents

Bill Kirchen.. 1
Bob Wootton... 2
Brian Setzer... 3
Buzz Campbell.. 5
Clyde Allen Hendrix... 6
Danny Gatton... 7
Don Gililland.. 9
Duke Robillard... 9
Eddie Bond.. 11
Eddie Cochran... 11
Ervin Williams... 14
Gene Summers... 14
Glen Glenn (singer).. 16
James Burton.. 16
Jesse Dayton... 18
Johnny Carroll... 18
Luther Perkins... 19
Rocky Burnette... 21
Rosie Flores... 21
Scotty Moore.. 22
Sonny Fisher.. 23
Tommy Allsup... 23

Preface

Each chapter in this book ends with a URL to a hyperlinked online version. Use the online version to access related pages, websites, footnotes, tables, color photos, updates, or to see the chapter's contributors. Click the edit link to suggest changes. Please type the URL exactly as it appears. If you change the URL's capitalization, for example, it may not work.

Purchase of this book entitles you to a free trial membership in the publisher's book club at www.booksllc.net. (Time limited offer.) Simply enter the barcode number from the back cover onto the membership form on our home page. The book club entitles you to select from millions of books at no additional charge, including a digital copy of this and related books to read on the go. Simply enter the title or subject onto the search form to find them.

If you have any questions, could you please be so kind as to consult our Frequently Asked Questions page at www.booksllc.net/faqs.cfm? You are also welcome to contact us there.

Publisher: Books LLC, Wiki Series, Memphis, TN, USA, 2012.

Bill Kirchen

Bill Kirchen

Kirchen in Shirlington, Virginia with his original telecaster in 2003

Background information

Born	June 29, 1948 Bridgeport, Connecticut
Origin	Bridgeport, CT U.S.
Genres	Rockabilly, Country music, Blues, Rock and Roll, jazz, Bakersfield Sound
Years active	1967–present

Labels Hightone Records

Bill Kirchen (born June 29, 1948) is an American rockabilly guitarist, singer and songwriter. He was a member of Commander Cody and His Lost Planet Airmen from 1967 to the mid-1970s and is known as "The Titan of The Telecaster" for his musical prowess on the guitar.

Early life

Kirchen was born in Bridgeport, CT but grew up in Ann Arbor, Michigan where he attended Ann Arbor High School and learned to play the trombone. He met a folksinger named David Siglin and joined the local folk scene. While learning to play banjo and guitar his musical interest began to extend beyond folk music and included the blues and various string bands. During his student days at University of Michigan, Ann Arbor, Kirchen started a "psycho folk-rock" band and later a country band that included George Frayne and John Tichy which formed the basis for the Commander Cody & His Lost Planet Airmen band.

Career

On stage, Alden Theater, McLean Virginia (2004)

In 1969 Kirchen took Commander Cody and the Lost Planet Airmen to California and they developed a reputation as musical "outlaws" that were praised by other outlaw musicians and bands like Willie Nelson, Waylon Jennings, The Grateful Dead and the Allman Brothers Band. Kirchen's band "played a collection of rock 'n' roll, hard-core country, boogie and rockabilly sounds produced in a "high-octane mix" that made them a "happening" group in the San Francisco Bay area

Kirchen began to develop as guitarist, vocalist, songwriter and performer. He became known for his vocal and guitar work on such songs as "Mama Hated Diesels", "Down to Seeds and Stems Again Blues" from the band's albums, *Hot Licks, Cold Steel & Truckers' Favorites* and *Lost in the Ozone*. His live performance work was captured on the 1973 album *Live From Deep in the Heart of Texas*, recorded at the Armadillo World Headquarters in 1973. Kirchen's Commander Cody band broke apart in 1976 and he formed a "swing orchestra" called the Moonlighters and began a decades long collaboration with British musician Nick Lowe. Lowe produced the Moonlighters second album titled "Rush Hour" and Kirchen toured with Lowe and joined him in the studio from time to time. During this period Kirchen also worked on albums with Elvis Costello, Gene Vincent, and Link Wray.

Around 1986 Kirchen moved to the Washington, D.C. area and formed the band, Too Much Fun with Dave Elliot on drums and John Previti on bass. In 1996 the band won 10 Washington Area Music Awards including Musician and Songwriter of the Year. Kirchen became a contemporary, and associate, of many D.C. guitarists such as the late Danny Gatton and Roy Buchanan, Link Wray, Tom Principato, Evan Johns, Billy Hancock, Linwood Taylor, Dave Chappell, Jimmy Thackery, the Nighthawks and others who, during this time, forged an elite fraternity of Washington D.C. area roots rock performers.

On stage Silver Spring, Maryland (2005)

Kirchen recorded the album *Tombstone Every Mile* on Demon Records, while in England and then released the recording in the USA after he signed with Black Top Records in 1994. He released the critically acclaimed and musically eclectic album, *Have Love, Will Travel* in 1996 and *Raise a Ruckus* on Hightone Records in 1999. Kirchen followed up with more album releases on Hightone Records including, *Tied to the Wheel* in 2001, *King of Dieselbilly* in 2005 and *Hammer of the Honkey-Tonk Gods* with Nick Lowe, Chris Gaffney and Dave Gonzalez in 2006. Other albums by Kirchen include: *Hot Rod Lincoln - Live* and *Dieselbilly Road Trip*.

Legacy

Kirchen is reported to be one of the musicians that pioneered the Americana radio format and is a founding father of the "twangcore movement" which includes Dave Alvin, Wilco and Big Sandy & His Fly-Rite Boys. Kirchen's signature sound has been dubbed "dieselbilly" and incorporates elements of Country music, Blues, Rockabilly, Western Swing and Boogie-Woogie, laced with themes of American truck driving music. Kirchen is said to have "one of the most distinctive, pure-Fender Telecaster tone guitar sounds in modern music".

Kirchen was named "The Titan of The Telecaster" by Guitar Player magazine for his musical prowess on the Fender Telecaster guitar. He plays a 1959 model with a maple fretboard and sunburst finish that was given to him in 1967 when he exchanged his Gibson SG with a stranger on a bus.

Personal life

Kirchen is a father and has been married for more than 25 years. In 2005 he moved to the West Coast and then to Manchaca, Texas. In early 2007 he returned to Maryland, then subsequently moved to Austin, Texas in 2011.

Source http://en.wikipedia.org/wiki/Bill_Kirchen

Bob Wootton

Bob Wootton is an American guitarist. He joined Johnny Cash's backing band, the Tennessee Three, after original lead guitarist, Luther Perkins, died in a house fire.

Biography

Wootton had been a lifelong fan of Cash's and played his songs religiously until he had perfected the boom-chicka-boom style known as Cash's unique sound. At one of Cash's shows, a flight cancellation left only Cash and drummer W.S. Holland onstage, and Wootton was asked to fill in. Wootton stunned the audience, particularly Cash himself, with perfect renditions of every song. Cash mentioned in passing that he might one day call on Wootton again, but within days asked him to join the tour as new lead guitarist.

One of the next performances, perhaps the most notable of Wootton's career, was at San Quentin State Prison where Cash's live album was recorded.

Wootton continued in the band with only a brief respite until Cash retired in 1997.

From 2006 to 2007, he performed with Cash's original drummer, W.S. Holland, his wife Vicky and daughter, Scarlett Wootton, as The Tennessee Three. In 2006 the band released their first album since Cash's death, a loving tribute titled "The Sound Must Go On."

The Tennessee Three was scheduled to perform at Folsom Prison in January 2008, commemorating the 40th anniversary of Cash's Folsom show. Wootton eventually withdrew from the concert project, which was later scrapped following disputes between prison officials and show promoters.

Wootton continued his 2008 touring as the Tennessee Three with drummer Derrick McCullough,, Vicky, Scarlett, and Montana Wootton to appreciative crowds across the globe. The band con-

Brian Setzer

Brian Setzer

Brian Setzer live in Salzburg, 2006

Background information

Born	April 10, 1959 Massapequa, New York, ed States
Genres	Rockabilly, rock and rol swing revival, jump blue
Occupations	Guitarist, musician, song
Instruments	Guitar, vocals
Years active	1979–present
Associated acts	The Brian Setzer Orches The Bloodless Pharoahs, Cats, The Tomcats
Website	www.briansetzer.com

Notable instruments

Gretsch Brian Setzer Signature Models

Brian Setzer (born April 10, 1959) is an American guitarist, singer and songwriter. He first found widespread success in the early 1980s with the 1950s-style rockabilly revival group Stray Cats, and revitalized his career in the late 1990s with his Swing revival band, The Brian Setzer Orchestra.

Biography

Career

Setzer was born in Massapequa, New York. Beginning in January 1979, he fronted the rockabilly band The Tomcats before transforming them into the later successful Stray Cats.

After performing locally from New York to Philadelphia under various band names with no real success, singer and lead guitarist Setzer, drummer Slim Jim Phantom (born James McDonnell) and bassist Lee Rocker (born Leon Drucker) decided in June 1980 to go to London, England where they believed people would better appreciate their sound and style.

To obtain the money for their plane tickets, Setzer, Rocker and Phantom went to Sam Ash Music on 48th Street to sell their instruments and gear to the store, for enough money for three one-way plane tickets. Upon their arrival, they decided to call themselves the "Stray Cats", a name suggested by Rocker because of their status as 'strays'. After performing for only a few months they drew the attention of the British record producer Dave Edmunds, and released a series of successful singles in the UK, which countered the already-entrenched punk scene in London.

After releasing several singles and two albums in England, the Stray Cats finally caught America's attention with the 1982 album *Built for Speed*, which included the two Top Ten hits, "Rock This Town" (#9) and "Stray Cat Strut" (#3). This album was basically a re-release of many of the songs from the two previous albums: the self-titled "Stray Cats" and "Gonna Ball" (they have never been released in America). Their follow-up 1983 album *Rant 'N Rave with the Stray Cats* included the two successful singles: "(She's) Sexy + 17" (#5), and "I Won't Stand In Your Way" (#35).

After only four years, the Stray Cats separated in 1984, but reunited briefly to record albums and mount tours several times all the way through the early 1990s. From 1985 to early 1986, Setzer was the lead guitarist for the touring version of Robert Plant's ensemble band, The Honeydrippers.

In the summer of 1986, Setzer released his first solo album, *The Knife Feels Like Justice*, which marked a huge move away from his trademark sound and towards a more mainstream 'rock-roots' sound, which was popularized at the time by such other artists such as John Cougar Mellencamp and Bruce Springsteen. The album was given little promotion by his label and as a result it only found minor success, peaking at only number 45 on the *Billboard* US album charts. The album has become a cult favorite among those who understood the message Setzer was trying to attempt, such as the world's nuclear proliferation, the immigration issue, the understanding of religion and the 'working man's blues', such as unemployment, loneliness, etc.

In 1987, Setzer played the part of Eddie Cochran in the biographical film on the life of Ritchie Valens, *La Bamba*.

Brian Setzer plays with his orchestra on June 29, 2006 in the East Room of the White House, during the entertainment following the official dinner in honor of Japanese Prime Minister Junichiro Koizumi's visit to the United States.

In the mid-1990s Setzer once again resurrected an older form of youth-oriented music, swing and jump blues music, when he formed The Brian Setzer Orchestra, an ambitious 17-piece ensemble project, which released four studio albums, a Christmas disc and several live releases between 1994 and 2002. His group's biggest success (and Setzer's outside the Stray Cats) came in 1998 with the release of the album *The Dirty Boogie* which cracked the top ten on the US album charts and featured a hit single, a cover of Louis Prima's "Jump, Jive an' Wail".

Setzer continued to release solo-billed albums sporadically, including a solo live disc *Rockin' By Myself* in 1998. In 2001 he released an album titled *Ignition* with his new trio billed as the '68 Comeback Special. In 2003 he released *Nitro Burnin' Funny Daddy*. A tribute album titled *Rockabilly Riot Vol. 1: A Tribute To Sun Records* was released on July 26, 2005, in the United States. An album simply titled *13* was released in October 2006.

On September 25, 2007, the Brian Setzer Orchestra released *Wolfgang's Big Night Out* which features Setzer's take on classical pieces, such as Beethoven's "Symphony No. 5" and "Für Elise". *Wolfgang* earned Setzer his eighth Grammy nomination, this time for Best Classical Crossover album of the year.

On October 13, 2009, the Brian Setzer Orchestra released a new album titled *Songs From Lonely Avenue*. For the first time in Setzer's career, he was the sole writer on every song. Frank Comstock, the 87-year-old big band arranger whom Setzer collaborated with on *Wolfgang's Big Night Out,* orchestrated most of the horn parts for the album.

On December 14, 2009, Setzer was unable to complete a performance in Albuquerque, New Mexico, and was briefly hospitalized because of "dehydration, high altitude sickness and vertigo," After Colorado Springs, Albuquerque has the second highest elevation of any American city of more than 100,000 people and many visitors experience oxygen debt and require ER treatment.

Recent activity

In 2011, Setzer toured extensively throughout Europe. The premiere night of *The Brian Setzer Rockabilly Riot! Europe Tour 2011* was at the 10 year celebration of the Azkena Rock Festival on the June 25, Vitoria Gasteiz, Spain to crowds of over 50,000 people.

The tour then went onto dates in Zurich, Switzerland; Luxembourg City, Luxembourg; Weert and Amsterdam in the Netherlands; Berlin, Hamburg and Cologne in Germany; and Peer in Belgium. The Scandinavia leg of the tour was in Copenhagen, Denmark, Stockholm, Sweden and Helsinki, Finland

Johan Frandsen, frontman from Swedish band The Knockouts and Brian Setzer on stage at the Helsinki Ice Hall, Finland, July 2011 as part of the European leg of the *Brian Setzer Rockabilly Riot 2011*

ending at the Helsinki Ice Hall.

Further gigs were held at the famous Brixton Academy, London and in Ireland, Dublin, the tour is planned to continue into Japan in September 2011. *The Brian Setzer Rockabilly Riot Tour!* featured a special set with Slim Jim Phantom, and was supported on the majority shows by the cult Swedish punk rock band The Knockouts in Germany, Denmark, Sweden and Finland.

Honors

Setzer was awarded the Orville H. Gibson Lifetime Achievement Award at the 1999 Gibson Awards. As of 1999, the previous recipients of this award were B. B. King, Emmylou Harris, Vince Gill and John Fogerty.

Since 2000, Setzer has earned three Grammy Awards: Best Pop Performance Duo/Group for "Jump Jive An' Wail", and two Best Pop Instrumental Performance awards for "Sleep Walk" and "Caravan". In December 2006 he received his seventh Grammy nomination for his version of "My Favorite Things", again in the Best Pop Instrumental Performance category.

Personal life

Setzer has been married three times: DeAnna Morgan from 1984 to 1992, with whom he has a son, Cody; Christine Schmidt, from 1994 to 2002, with whom he has two daughters; and Julie Reiten, a former singer with the Dustbunnies, in 2005 (they met when she auditioned - and was hired - as a back-up singer for the Brian Setzer Orchestra in 2000). Setzer and Reiten reside in Minneapolis.

Discography

Bloodless Pharaohs

Marty Thau Presents 2 × 5 (1980)
Brian Setzer and the Bloodless Pharaohs (1996, Collectables 687)

Brian Setzer & The Tomcats

A series of live recordings were issued in 1997 by Collectables Records, and removed from sale within a year under threat of legal action.
Rock This Town (Recorded Live on March 29, 1980) (Collectables 701)
High School Confidential (Recorded Live on May 24, 1980) (Collectables 702)
Stray Cat Strut (Recorded Live on May 24, 1980) (Collectables 703)
Rip It Up! (Recorded Live on May 30, 1980) (Collectables 704)
All Shook Up (Recorded Live on May 30, 1980) (Collectables 705)
Shake Rattle & Roll (Recorded Live on May 31, 1980) (Collectables 706)
Rockabilly Boogie (Recorded Live on October 10, 1980) (Collectables 707)

Stray Cats

Stray Cats (1981)
Gonna Ball (1981)
Built For Speed (1982) No. 2 (15 weeks) US
Rant N' Rave with the Stray Cats (1983) No. 14 US
Rock Therapy (1986) No. 122 US
Blast Off! (1989) No. 111 US
Let's Go Faster! (1990)
The Best of the Stray Cats: Rock This Town (1990)
Choo Choo Hot Fish (1992)
Original Cool (1993)
Rumble in Brixton (2004)

The Brian Setzer Orchestra

The Brian Setzer Orchestra (1994) No. 158 US
Guitar Slinger (1996)
The Dirty Boogie (1998) No. 9 US
Vavoom! (2000) No. 62 US
Jumpin' East of Java (2001)
Best of The Big Band (2002)

Boogie Woogie Christmas (2002)
The Ultimate Collection (2004)
Dig That Crazy Christmas (2005)
Wolfgang's Big Night Out (September 2007)
The Best Of Collection - Christmas Rocks! (October 2008)
Ultimate Christmas Collection (October 2008)
Songs from Lonely Avenue (October 2009)
Don't Mess With A Big Band (Live!) (July 2010)
Christmas Comes Alive (October 2010)

Solo material

The Knife Feels Like Justice (1986) No. 45 US
Live Nude Guitars (1988) No. 140 US
Rockin' By Myself (1998)
Nitro Burnin' Funny Daddy (2003)
Rockabilly Riot Vol. 1: A Tribute To Sun Records (2005)
13 (2006) No. 2 JAP
Red Hot & Live (2007)
Setzer Goes Instru-MENTAL! (2011)

'68 Comeback special

Ignition (2001) No. 152 US

Filmography

La Bamba (1987)
Mother Goose Rock 'n' Rhyme (1990)
The Great White Hype (1996)
The Nanny - "The Bobbi Flekman Story'" (1997), as himself
The Country Bears (2002), along with the '68 Comeback Special
The Simpsons - "How I Spent My Strummer Vacation" (2002)

Live DVDs

Brian Setzer Orchestra live In Japan (2001)
Rumble In Brixton (2004)
Brian Setzer Orchestra Live: Christmas Extravaganza (2005)
One Rockin' Night ('95) (2007)
Live In Montreal Jazz Festival (2010)

Other works and appearances

Performed the guitar solo on the Twisted Sister song *Be Chrool to Your Scuel*. Composed and performed the theme song for the Disney cartoon show *House Of Mouse*.
Appeared in a Bud Light commercial where his rehearsal session was interrupted by an elderly woman (recording pioneer Cordell Jackson) who could play rock-and-roll guitar.
Setzer also performed on Tomoyasu Hotei's album *Soul Sessions*, on the tracks *Back Streets of Tokyo* and *Take a Chance on Love*.
Appeared with the Brian Setzer Orchestra on an episode of The Nanny *The Bobbi Flekman Story* (1997)
Setzer spoofed himself in a 2002 episode of popular animated series The Simpsons. He voiced himself as a "tutor" at a fictional Rock 'n Roll Fantasy Camp attended by Homer Simpson, and said (after his animated version participated in chasing Homer in a motorized devil's head): "I hope you won't judge the entire Brian Setzer Orchestra based on my actions."
Appeared in The Country Bears Movie doing a music duel with one of the bears.

Musical equipment

Brian Setzer has a very large guitar collection spanning many decades and brands. Setzer favours vintage equipment and hollow body guitars and is currently endorsed by Gretsch.

Vintage guitars:	Signature guitars:
D'Angelico Excel - 1938	Gretsch Model 6120 Setzer Signature Prototype
D'Angelico New Yorker - 1940	Gretsch Model 6120 Setzer Hot Rod Custom Purple
Martin Model D-28 Acoustic - 1956	
Fender Stratocaster Turquoise - 1957	Gretsch Model 6120 Setzer Hot Rod Custom "Pinstripe"
Guild Bluesbird - 1959	Gretsch Model 6120 Setzer Hot Rod Custom "Spotty"
Gretsch Model 6130 Round Up - 1955	
Gretsch Model 6128 Black Duo Jet - 1957	Gretsch Model 6120 Setzer Hot Rod Custom "Sparkle Red"
Gretsch Model 6136 White Falcon - 1957	Gretsch Model 6120 Setzer Hot Rod Custom "Sparkle Blue"
Gretsch Model 6129 Silver Jet - No Pickguard - 1957	Gretsch Model 6120 SSLVO Brian Setzer Signature
Gretsch Model 6129 Silver Jet - White Pickguard - 1957	Gretsch Model 6120 SSL Brian Setzer Signature
Gretsch Model 6136 White Falcon - 1957	Gretsch Model 6120 SSU Brian Setzer Signature
Gretsch Model 6129 Silver Jet - Black Pickguard - 1958	Gretsch Model 6120 SSUGR Brian Setzer Signature
Gretsch Model 6120 "Stray Cat" - 1959	Gretsch Model 6136SLBP Brian Setzer Black Phoenix Indie Model With White GT Stripes
Gretsch Model 6120 Chet Atkins - 1959	
Gretsch Model 6119 "Christmas Custom" - 1959	Other guitars: Bigsby Custom - 2003
Gretsch Model 6119 Blue Sparkle Jet - 1959	Effects: Roland Re-301 Chorus Echo
Gretsch Model 6120 - 1960	Amplifiers: Fender Bassman - 1962
Gretsch Model 6119 - 1960	Fender Princeton
Gibson Firebird V - 1964	

Source http://en.wikipedia.org/wiki/Brian_Setzer

Buzz Campbell

Buzz Campbell is an American guitarist, vocalist and songwriter. He plays anything that is close to Rockabilly music, Blues, Swing, Country & Rock & roll. Buzz Campbell is also a renown song writer. He has played with numerous "rockabilly acts", including Lee Rocker, Slim Jim Phantom and Brian Setzer, all original members of the Stray Cats. Buzz Campbell and his group have also backed up and performed with such artists as Chuck Berry, Jerry Lee Lewis, Willie Nelson, Bo Diddley, Chris Isaac, and numerous others and has become a mainstay on the California rockabilly scene. He is now touring all over the American soil, in Canada and has a solid international reputation.

The early years

Buzz Campbell was born on January 19, 1969, in Dallas, Texas. He was first introduced to 1950s doo-wop by his father's old cassettes. He soon thereafter picked up the guitar, and with the influence of his uncle, began to learn 1950s-style rock and roll. At first it was just a hobby, but in 1991 at his twenty-first Birthday, he saw the Stray Cats perform live at the Bacchanal in San Diego, Calif. The show had such an impact on him that he dropped out of college, to concentrate on the music.

Buzz Campbell has named Chuck Berry as his first reel influence and later came Carl Perkins, Cliff Gallup, Scotty Moore, James Burton and the one he said was his biggest influence would be Brian Setzer, of the Stray Cats.

Career

In 2001, Buzz was approached at a gig by Jocko Marcellino, one of the founding members of the 1950s group, Sha Na Na (2000–2004). This group is internationally known for their debut at Woodstock, their TV show in the mid-'70s, and their cameo in the cult classic movie *Grease*. Buzz became the lead guitarist for Sha Na Na, and still occasionally performs with them. In 1995 Buzz also participated in the groupe called "The Bastard Sons Of Johnny Cash(They are now called: Mark Stuart and The Bastard Sons)", on the lead guitar. More than 10 years ago, Buzz was given the opportunity to open for Lee Rocker.(Present on both albums: Racin' the Devil and Black Cat Bone.) Buzz even wrote the track, "Crazy When She Drinks" for the Black Cat Bone album. Buzz and Lee met and a long standing friendship started. Lee was impressed and produced Hot Rod Lincoln's critically acclaimed CD titled "Blue Café." Buzz Campbell completed his largest tour to date by opening for the Stray Cats European Farwell Tour in the summer of 2008. The band warmed up audiences in seven different countries and by the end of the tour, were seen by over 100,000 people. Buzz is a master of rockabilly, roots country, blues, and roots rock styles.

The Gear

Buzz Campbell is sponsored by Gretsch. He uses mostly a 2007, 6136 Gretsch White Falcon .
Also has a 1958 Gretsch Country Club(mostly for recording on the RHL and Lee Rocker albums).
On live performances, he as used a 90s red Gretsch Hot Rod.
When writing songs, he also uses a Gibson acoustic.

Albums

Hot Rod Lincoln

Blue Cafe(1999)
Astraunaut Girl(2001)
Tokyo Bop(2003)
RunAway Girl(2006)
The Best of Buzz Campbell & Hotrodlincoln(2008)

Lee Rocker

Racin' the Devil(2006)
Black Cat Bone(2007)

Buzz Campbell Band

Buzz Campbell: Shivers & Shakes(2010)

Source http://en.wikipedia.org/wiki/Buzz_Campbell

Clyde Allen Hendrix

Clyde Allen Hendrix (Al Hendrix) is an American rockabilly singer and songwriter.

Career

He was born November 12, 1934. He began performing in clubs around Bakersfield, California, and met Buck Owens at the legendary Blackboard Cafe. Al and Buck made music together, often with Bill Woods and The Orange Blossom Playboys. Hendrix made his television debut on the Los Angeles based show "Rocket To Stardom."

In 1957, Joe Keplinger (a.k.a Jolly Jody) hired Al as lead singer for his group, Jolly Jody and The Go Daddies. With the Go Daddies, Al recorded "Rhonda Lee" and "Go Daddy Rock" for the Tally label. The two singles were picked up by ABC Paramount in 1959. Hendrix also appeared on Cousin Herb Henson's TV show, "Trading Post Gang".

LaGree Records issued "I Need You" and "Young and Wild" in 1960. Liberty Records leased them for nationwide release. "I Need You" was a number one hit in El Paso, Texas for 6 weeks. Around the same time, Alan Freed played the flipside "Young and Wild" every hour on his radio show in Los Angeles. "I Need You" also made the top 20 in San Diego.

Hendrix appeared on the Wink Martindale television show at Pacific Ocean Beach and at Art Laboe's show at Pasadena Civic Auditorium.

"Monkey Bite" and "For Sentimental Reasons" were released in 1962 on Pike Records. "Monkey Bite" was banned from some radio stations for being too risqué. Two more tracks recorded at Pike, "Jumpin' Johnny" and "Fooling Around" were not issued until 1985 on the White label in Holland.

Hendrix appeared on early Bakersfield television shows hosted by Jimmy Thomason. His band Al and The Country Mixers performed on radio, TV, and at entertainment centers in the area.

In 1971, he released two more songs

on LaGree, "Georgia Kate" and "Wait Until You Get a Whiff of My After Shave Lotion" (also called "Mixing Fun" and "Shaving lotion".)

In 2003, Bear Family Records issued *That'll Flat Git It: Volume 13: Rockabilly From The Vaults Of ABC Records* which includes the Al Hendrix song "Rhonda Lee". Al Hendrix songs also are in various artist collections from Buffalo Bop Records, World Music Distribution, Lucky, Teen Beat, Membran Music, and Mustang Records.

In 2007 Hummingbird Records released new Hendrix originals "Good Girl I Ain't Got", "When I'm loving You", "Rainbow's End", "Diabetic Man", "The DJ", "I Can Tell", "Cock Fighter", and "The Answer To It All" on the CD *Rare and Rockin'*, along with some of his older material.

In 2009 Hendrix came out with *Rockabilly Lovin'*, a CD of all new original songs. A love songs CD, *Lover Boy*, is being released in 2012.

Al Hendrix was recognized as a Rockabilly Legend by the Rockabilly Hall of Fame in 2008.

Al Hendrix performed at Buck Owens' Crystal Palace in Bakersfield on February 13, 2010. He performed at the Viva Las Vegas rockabilly festival in April, 2011.

Discography

"Rhonda Lee" and "Go Daddy Rock" (ABC Paramount 1959)
"I Need You" and "Young and Wild" (Liberty Records 1960)
"Monkey Bite" and "For Sentimental Reasons" (Pike Records 1962)
"Georgia Kate" and "Wait Until You Get a Whiff of My After Shave Lotion" (LaGree Records 1971)
"Jumpin' Johnny" and "Fooling Around' (White Label 1985)
Teenage Repression (Various Artists, World Music Distribution 1993)
Young and Wild (Various Artists, Buffalo Bop Records 1994)
Rockabilly Gold, Volume 3 (Various Artists, Lucky Records 1996)
That'll Flat Git It: Volume 13: Rockabilly From The Vaults Of ABC Records (Bear Family Records 2003)
Play It Cool (Various Artists, Teen Beat Records 2004)
Rock-A-Billy, Rock and Roll & Hillbilly (Various Artists, Membran Music 2011)
Rockin' Jive & Stroll, Volume 12: Oh Oh Rock! (Various Artists, Mustang Records)
Rare and Rockin' (Hummingbird Records 2007)
Rockabilly Lovin' (Hummingbird Records 2009)
Lover Boy (Hummingbird Records 2012)
Source http://en.wikipedia.org/wiki/Clyde_Allen_Hendrix

Danny Gatton

Danny Gatton	
Birth name	Daniel Wood Gatton
Born	September 4, 1945 Washington, D.C.
Died	October 4, 1994 (aged 49) Newburg, Maryland
Genres	Blues, rockabilly, jazz
Occupations	Musician
Instruments	Guitar
Years active	1960–1994
Website	www.dannygatton.com
Notable instruments	
Fender Telecaster	

Danny Gatton (September 4, 1945 – October 4, 1994) was an American guitarist who fused rockabilly, jazz, and country styles to create his own distinctive style of playing. A biography, *Unfinished Business: The Life and Times of Danny Gatton* by Ralph Heibutzki, was published in 2003. It has a voluminous discography. Gatton was ranked 63rd on *Rolling Stone* magazine's 100 Greatest Guitarists of all Time in 2003. On May 26, 2010, Gibson.com ranked Gatton as the 27th best guitarist of all time.

Early life

Gatton was born in Washington, D.C. on September 4, 1945. His father, Daniel W. Gatton Sr., was a rhythm guitarist known for his unique percussive style, who left his musical career to raise his family in a more stable profession. The younger Gatton grew up to share his father's passion for the instrument.

Career

Danny Gatton began his career playing in bands while still a teenager. He began to attract wider interest in the 1970s while playing guitar and banjo for the group Liz Meyer & Friends. He made his name as a performer in the Washington, DC, area during the late 1970s and 1980s, both as a solo performer and with his Redneck Jazz Explosion, in which he would trade licks with virtuoso pedal steel player Buddy Emmons over a tight bass-drums rhythm which drew from blues, country, bebop and rockabilly influences. He also backed Robert Gordon and Roger Miller. He contributed a cover of "Apricot Brandy", a song by Elektra Records-supergroup Rhinoceros, to the 1990 compilation album *Rubáiyát*.

Playing style

Gatton's playing combined musical styles such as jazz, blues and rockabilly in an innovative fashion, and he was known by some as "the Telemaster." He was also called "the world's greatest unknown guitarist". His most common nickname was "The Humbler", owing to his ability to "humble" or out-play anyone willing to go up against him in "head-cutting" jam sessions. It was Amos Garrett, guitar player for Maria Muldaur, who nicknamed Gatton "The Humbler". After a successful gig, Garrett would pull out a tape of Gatton and tell his band, "You think we played well tonight. Let's take a minute to listen to the Humble-lizer." A photo published in the October 2007 issue of *Guitar Player* magazine shows Gatton playing in front of a neon sign that says "Victims Wanted".

However, he never achieved the commercial success that his talent arguably deserved. His album *88 Elmira Street* was up for a 1990 Grammy Award for the song "Elmira Street Boogie" in the category *Best Rock Instrumental Performance*, but was beaten by Eric Johnson with "Cliffs of Dover".

His skills were most appreciated by his peers such as Eric Clapton, Willie Nelson, Steve Earle, and his childhood idol Les Paul. During his career, Gatton appeared on stage with guitar heroes such as Alvin Lee and Jimmie Vaughan, the latter literally walking in one night on a Gatton club gig. There is also an apocryphal rumor about an on-stage "head-cutting" jam between Gatton and fellow Washington DC-area resident (and Telecaster player who also held the title of The Greatest Unknown Guitarist) Roy Buchanan. (Gatton had roomed with Buchanan in Nashville, Tennessee in the mid '60s and they became frequent "jamming partners", according to *Guitar Player* magazine's October 2007 issue). He also performed with old teenage friend Jack Casady and Jorma Kaukonen (from Jefferson Airplane and Hot Tuna) as "Jack and the Degenerates". Those recordings were never commercially released, but live tapes are in circulation. In 1993, Gatton was invited by rocker Chris Isaak to record tracks for Isaak's *San Francisco Days* CD. Reports of where Gatton's playing can be heard on the CD vary, with unconfirmed reports placing him on either "Can't Do a Thing (To Stop Me)", "5:15" or "Beautiful Houses". Gatton reportedly brought a customized Fender Telecaster and Stratocaster to the recording session.

He usually played a 1953 Fender Telecaster (Fender now manufactures a replica of his heavily customized instrument), with Joe Barden pick-ups and Fender Super 250L's, or Nickel Plated Steel (.010 to .046 with a .015 for the G) strings. For a slide, Gatton was known for using a beer bottle or mug (still half full of beer), without regard to whether it might spill all over stage or his guitar.

During a 1991 performance on *Austin City Limits*, he followed this by wiping the guitar neck with a rag, then holding the rag between his fingers and the frets, all the while playing flawlessly. In the March 1989 issue of *Guitar Player* magazine, he said he preferred to use an Alka-Seltzer bottle or long 6L6 vacuum tube as a slide, but that audiences liked the beer bottle. He did, however, only play slide overhand, citing his earlier training in steel guitar [Guitar Player, March 1989]

He always played with a jazz-style teardrop pick, and was capable of intricate passages combining Bluegrass, bebop, and garage sounds, executed with amazing clarity and at dizzying speeds. His picking technique was a hybrid combination of pick and fingers, primarily his middle and ring fingers on his right hand. The basis of his picking technique was using banjo rolls; he was an accomplished banjo player and from that he learned the traditional (Scruggs style) right-hand technique. His forward roll consisted of a pick downstroke, then middle finger, then ring finger. His backward roll consisted of middle finger, then a pick upstroke, then a pick downstroke. He possessed a classical guitar left hand technique, thumb behind the neck, fretting with arched fingers.

Also among his admirers are Les Paul, James Burton, Lenny Breau, Joe Bonamassa (whom Danny mentored when Joe was eleven years old), Vince Gill, Evan Johns (of Evan Johns and His H-Bombs), Chris Cheney, Bill Kirchen, Albert Lee, Steve Vai, Buckethead, Arlen Roth, Johnny Hiland, Ricky Skaggs, Slash (Guns N' Roses), and Richie Sambora.

Suicide

On October 4, 1994, Gatton locked himself in his garage in Newburg, Maryland and shot himself. He left behind no explanation. In retrospect of his suicide, people around him have suggested that he may have gone in and out of depression for many years.

On January 10, 11, and 12, 1995, Tramps club in New York organized a three-night tribute to Danny Gatton featuring dozens of Gatton's musical admirers, the highlight of which was a twenty-minute performance by Les Paul, James Burton, and Albert Lee. Those shows (with all musicians performing for free) raised $25,000 for Gatton's widow and daughter.

Discography

1975 – *American Music*
1978 – *Redneck Jazz*
1987 – *Unfinished Business*
1990 – *Blazing Telecasters* (live April 27, 1984)
1991 – *88 Elmira St.*
1992 – *New York Stories* with Joshua Redman, Roy Hargrove, Bobby Watson, & Franck Amsallem
1993 – *Cruisin' Deuces*
1994 – *Relentless* (with Joey DeFrancesco)
1995 – *Redneck Jazz Explosion* (live December 30 & 31, 1978)
1996 – *The Humbler* (with Robert Gordon)
1998 – *In Concert 9/9/94*
1998 – *Untouchable*
1998 – *Portraits*
1999 – *Anthology*
2004 – *Funhouse* (live June 10 & 11, 1988)
2005 – *Oh No! More Blazing Guitars* (with Tom Principato)
2006 – *Redneck Jazz Explosion, Vol. 2* (live December 30 & 31, 1978)
2007 – *Live in 1977: The Humbler Stakes His Claim*
2011 – *Blue Skies Calling*, a CD by Boy Wells includes nearly an hour of Gatton and Wells playing in his living room. "Danny called me before he died and asked me to put a vocal tape together for his label at the time. He needed a singer after his singer, Billy Windsor, had passed. He remained a friend, a good one all those years. This lesson was in the late '70s; it's me and Danny in the living room of his house on Holly Lane in Indian Head, Maryland. It's killer stuff."

Source   http://en.wikipedia.org/wiki/Danny_Gatton

Don Gililland

Don Dow Gililland (commonly misspelled as **Gilliland**; born 31 January 1939 Dallas, Texas) is a jazz guitarist and composer who is best known for having recorded three rockabilly hits in 1956 on Sun Records with "Wade & Dick — The College Kids," led by Wade Lee Moore (born 1934) and Dick Penner:

> *Wild Woman*
> *Don't Need Your Lovin'*
> *Bop Bop Baby*

Bop Bop Baby was included on the soundtrack of *Walk the Line*, the film biography of Johnny Cash. Gililland has been legally blind since birth but has always been able to get around. Gililland played guitar with Buster Smith. Gililland also worked 26 years for the *Oak Cliff Tribune*, becoming managing editor. He currently works for Dallas Area Rapid Transit and still performs in the evenings.

Selected discography

Jazz

One O'Clock Lab Band
Recorded in Denton, Texas, released in 1961 by 90th Floor Records SSL907 OCLC 15010703
Re-released as a compilation in 2005 by 90th Floor Records SSL907
Re-released in 2009 under the title *The Road to Stan* as a tribute to various performances by musicians who later were associated with the Stan Kenton Orchestra by 90th Floor Records SSL907 OCLC 501846239
Marvin Stamm, Ron Towell, John Crews, Tom Wirtel, John Inglis (trumpets), Morgan Powell (lead), Dee Barton, William Barton, Larry Moser, Jerry Schulze (trombones), David Irving, Bill Pickering (french horns), John La Forge (tuba), Ken Fears (flute), Archie Wheeler (lead alto sax), Allan Solganick (alto sax), Jerry Keys (tenor, flute), Ray Kireilis (tenor & bari sax), Herb Porter (bari sax & bass clarinet), Lanny Steele (piano), Don Gililland (electric guitar), Toby Guynn (bass), Paul Guerrero (drums), Leon Breeden (conductor)
Don Jacoby, *Swinging Big Sound: Don Jacoby and The College All Stars*
Recorded in Chicago, October 1961
Released by Decca DL4241 (mono), DL74241 (stereo) OCLC 8983410
Gary Slavo, Tom Wirtel, Bob Clull, Chris Witherspoon (trumpets), Don Jacoby (trumpet, leader), Dee Barton, William Barton, Loren Binford, Dave Wheeler (trombones), Al Beutler, John Giordano (alto sax), Jerry Keys (alto & bari sax), Bob Pierson, Don Melka (tenor sax), Keith Jarrett (piano), Don Gililland (guitar), Toby Guynn (bass), John Von Ohlen (drums)

Rockabilly

Wade & Dick – The College Kids
Recorded at Pepper Studio (Sun Studio), 706 Union Avenue, Memphis, December 14, 1956
Sun Records 269 (released May 27, 1957)
Bop Bop Baby (BMI U-250)
backed with ("bw") *Don't Need Your Lovin Baby* (BMI U-251)
Bob Izer plays guitar, Gililland plays bass
Sun Records (released 1956)
Bop Bop Baby (alternate version) (BMI U-250)
backed with ("bw") *Wild Woman*
Dick Penner
Recorded at Pepper Studio (Sun Studio), 706 Union Avenue, Memphis, February 16, 1957
Sun Records 282
Cindy Lou (BMI U-279)
Gililland plays guitar
Restless (neo-rockabilly band)
> *Sag, Drag and Fall*
Musical score for *Sag, Drag and Fall* composed by Ken Massey & Don Gililland (© 1955) OCLC 495081157
Recording released in 1987 by Nervous Records, *Restless – The Early Years 1981-83*
Re-released in 2001 by Be Be's Records, *Restless – The Nervous Years*
Re-released by Documents, Membran Music Ltd., *Various – Early Rock 'N' Roll And Rockabilly*

Filmography

Rock Baby, Rock It! (video sample)
Executive producer: J.G. Tiger (né Jack David Goldman; 1929–2000)
Director: Murray Douglas Sporup (1922–1995)
Premier: 21 March 1957, Dallas
Gililland plays Ronnie, a bespectacled guitarist in the film
Source http://en.wikipedia.org/wiki/Don_Gililland

Duke Robillard

Duke Robillard

Robillard in 2006. Photograph: Louis R

Background information

Birth name	Michael John Robillard
Born	October 4, 1948 Woonsocket, Rhode Island, United States
Genres	Blues, blues rock, rockabilly, swing jazz
Occupations	Musician, songwriter, ba
Instruments	Vocals, guitar
Years active	1967–1990 Roomful of 1990–1993: The Fabulous derbirds 1993–present: (Duke Ro Band)
Labels	Stony Plain Records, Ch records, Rounder Recor Top Records, Point Blan

Associated acts	Records, Flying Fish Records, Flying Fish Records, Columbia Records Duke Robillard Band, Roomful of Blues, The Fabulous Thunderbirds
Website	Duke Robillard.com

Michael John "Duke" Robillard (born October 4, 1948, Woonsocket, Rhode Island) is an American blues musician.

After playing in various bands and working for the Guild Guitar Company, he co-founded the band Roomful of Blues with pianist Al Copley in 1967. He has also been a member of The Fabulous Thunderbirds which included Kim Wilson, replacing Jimmie Vaughan on guitar. Also experienced in jazz, swing, and rock and roll, aside from his preferred blues music, Robillard has been generally regarded as a guitar player keeping the blues style of T-Bone Walker.

He has recorded with artists such as Jimmy Witherspoon, Snooky Prior, Jay McShann, Hal Singer, Pinetop Perkins, Joe Louis Walker, Todd Sharpville, Tom Waits and Bob Dylan. In the summer of 2006, Robillard accompanied Tom Waits on a tour of the Southern United States.

Session work

Robillard has contributed to a large number of musicians' recordings in his career. Some of the most famous have been mentioned, but others include artists as diverse as Wham! and Jimmy Witherspoon.

Robillard was hired by Tom Waits, who was looking for a blues guitarist and a master of American roots music for his Orphans Tour. Although Robillard did not record with Waits, the 2006 dates were widely bootlegged. Robillard's latest album *Tales from the Tiki Lounge*, was a tribute to Les Paul, and he played an array of Gold Tops and other Les Paul models, plus an Epiphone Broadway.

Awards

He has been nominated for and has received numerous awards over his career. Awards include:
2007 Rhode Island Pell Award for Excellence in the Arts
2001 "Best Blues Guitarist" W.C. Handy Award
2000 "Best Blues Guitarist" W.C. Handy Award
Robillard has also been nominated for:
2007 "Best Contemporary Blues Album" for "Guitar Groove-A-Rama" Grammy Award
2010 "Best Traditional Blues Album" for "Stomp! The Blues Tonight" Grammy Award

Discography

Duke Robillard Performing in May 2012

Roomful of Blues - Roomful of Blues (1978)
Let's Have a Party - Roomful of Blues (1979)
Duke Robillard & The Pleasure Kings (1984) (Rounder Records)
Too Hot to Handle (1985) (Rounder)
Swing (1987) (Rounder)
You Got Me (1988) (Rounder)
Soul Searchin' - Ronnie Earl and the Broadcasters (1988) (Black Top Records)
Soul Deep - Miki Honeycutt (1989) (Rounder)
Rockin' Blues (1988) (Rounder)
Royal Blue - Al Copley and Hal Singer (1990) (Modern Blues)
Heavy Juice - Greg Piccolo (1990) (Black Top Records)
Turn it Around (1991) (Rounder)
Too Cool to Move - with Snooky Pryor (1991) (Antones Records)
Poison Kisses - with Jerry Portnoy (1991) (Modern Blues)
Texas Bluesman - with Zuzu Bollin (1991) (Antones Records)
After Hours Swing Session (1992) (Rounder)
Pinetop's Boogie Woogie - with Pinetop Perkins (1992) (Antones Records)
Good Understanding - with Al Copley and the Fabulous Thunderbirds (1993) (Suffering Egos Records)
Toolin' Around - with Arlen Roth (1993) (Blue Plate Records)
Minor Swing - Gerry Beaudoin and David Grisman (1994) (North Star Records)
Temptation (1994) (Point Blank Records)
Spoon's Blues - Jimmy Witherspoon (1995) (Stony Plain Records)
Get Down with the Blues - Tony Z (1995) (Tone Cool Records)
Married to the Blues - with Mark Hummel (1995) (Flying Fish Records)
Duke's Blues (1996) (Virgin Records)
Found True Love - with John Hammond (1996) (Point Blank Records)
Dangerous Place (1997) (Point Blank Records)
Hootie's Jumpin' Blues - with Jay McShann (1997) (Stony Plain Records)
Time out of Mind - with Bob Dylan (1997) (Columbia Records)
Duke Robillard Plays Jazz (1997) (Rounder)
Duke Robillard Plays Blues (1997) (Rounder)
Stretchin' Out Live (1998) (Stony Plain Records)
New Blues for Modern Man (1999) (Shanachie)
Jimmy Witherspoon with The Duke Robillard Band Jimmy Witherspoon (1999) (Stony Plain Records)
Explorer (2000) (Shanachie)
Living with the Blues (2000) (Stony Plain Records)
Still Jumpin' The Blues - Jay McShann (2000) (Stony Plain Records)
Blow Mr. Low - with Doug James (2001) (Stony Plain Records)

Retrospective - New Guitar Summit (2001) (Francesca Records)
Living With The Blues (2002) (Dixiefrog Records)
More Conversations in Swing Guitar (2002) (Stony Plain Records)
Exalted Lover (2003) (Stony Plain Records)
Blue Mood (2003) (Stony Plain Records)
New Guitar Summit (2004) - Jay Geils, Duke Robillard, Gerry Beaudoin (Stony Plain Records)
The Duke Meets The Earl - with Ronnie Earl (2005) (Stony Plain Records)
Guitar Groove-A-Rama (2006) (Stony Plain Records)
World of Blues (2007) (Stony Plain Records)
Duke's Box (2009) (Dixie Frog Records)
Sunny and Her Joy Boys with Duke Robillard (2009) (Stony Plain Records)
Stomp! The Blues Tonight (2009) (Stony Plain Records)
Porchlight with Todd Sharpville (2010) (MiG Music)
Passport to the Blues (2010) (Stony Plain Records)
Low Down And Tore Up (2011) (Stony Plain Records)
Source http://en.wikipedia.org/wiki/Duke_Robillard

Eddie Bond

Eddie Bond

Background information

Born	July 1, 1933 Memphis, Tennessee, United States
Occupations	Singer, musician
Years active	1950s–1990s
Labels	Mercury
Associated acts	Elvis Presley, Carl Perkins, Jerry Lee Lewis, Johnny Cash, Roy Orbison, Warren Smith

Eddie Bond (born July 1, 1933 in Memphis, Tennessee, United States) is an American pioneer singer and guitar player of American Rockabilly music.

In the mid 1950s, Bond recorded for Mercury Records and toured with Elvis Presley, Carl Perkins, Jerry Lee Lewis, Johnny Cash, Roy Orbison, Warren Smith and others. He is most infamous for having rejected the then 18-year-old Elvis Presley, who was auditioning for Bond's band. It was shortly thereafter that Presley recorded his first single at Sun Records.

Bond's contribution to the genre has been recognized by the Rockabilly Hall of Fame.

Source http://en.wikipedia.org/wiki/Eddie_Bond

Eddie Cochran

Eddie Cochran

Background information

Birth name	Ray Edward Cochran
Born	October 3, 1938 Albert Lea, Minnesota
Died	April 17, 1960 (aged 21) Bath, Somerset, England
Genres	Rock and roll, rockabilly
Occupations	Singer-songwriter, musician
Instruments	Guitar, vocals
Years active	1953–1960
Labels	Liberty

Notable instruments

Gretsch 6120

Ray Edward 'Eddie' Cochran (October 3, 1938–April 17, 1960) was an American rock and roll pioneer who, in his brief career, had a small but lasting influence on rock music through his guitar playing. Cochran's rockabilly songs, such as "C'mon Everybody", "Somethin' Else", and "Summertime Blues", captured teenage frustration and desire in the late 1950s and early 1960s. He experimented with multitrack recording and overdubbing even on his earliest singles, and was also able to play piano, bass and drums. His image as a sharply dressed, rugged but good-looking young man with a rebellious attitude epitomized the stance of the Fifties rocker, and in death he achieved an iconic status.

Cochran was born in Minnesota and moved with his family to California in the early 1950s. He was involved with music from an early age, playing in the school band and teaching himself to play blues guitar. In 1955 he formed a duet with the unrelated guitarist Hank Cochran, and when they split the following year, Cochran began a songwriting career with Jerry Capehart. His first success came when he performed the song "Twenty Flight Rock" in the movie *The Girl Can't Help It*, starring Jayne Mansfield. Soon afterward, Liberty Records signed him to a recording contract.

Cochran died aged 21 after a road accident in the town of Chippenham, Wiltshire, during his British tour in April 1960. Though his best-known songs were released during his lifetime, more of his songs were released posthumously. In 1987, Cochran was inducted into the Rock and Roll Hall of Fame. His songs have been much covered by bands such as The Who, The Beach Boys, The Beatles, Dick Dale & his Del-Tones, Blue Cheer, Led Zeppelin, Rush, Humble Pie, Commander Cody and His Lost Planet Airmen, Joan Jett and the Blackhearts, Teenage Head, Tiger Army, UFO, The White Stripes, Stray Cats, and the Sex Pistols.

Early life

Cochran was born in Albert Lea, Minnesota, as Ray Edward Cochran. His parents were from Oklahoma, and he always stated in interviews that he was from Oklahoma. He took music lessons in school but quit the band to play drums. Also, rather than taking piano lessons, he began learning guitar, playing the country music he heard on the radio.

Music career

Early career (1953-1956)

In 1953, Cochran's family moved to Bell Gardens, California. As his guitar playing improved, he formed a band with two friends from his junior high school. He dropped out of Bell Gardens High School in his first year to become a professional musician. During a show featuring many performers at an American Legion hall, he met Hank Cochran (later a country music songwriter). Although they were not related, they recorded as The Cochran Brothers and began performing together. Eddie Cochran also worked as a session musician and began writing songs, making a "demo" with Jerry Capehart, his future manager. In 1956, Boris Petroff asked Cochran if he would appear in the musical comedy film *The Girl Can't Help It*. He agreed, and sang a song called "Twenty Flight Rock" in the movie.

Later career (1957–1960)

In 1957 Cochran starred in his second film, *Untamed Youth*, and also had his first hit, "Sittin' in the Balcony", one of the few songs he recorded that were written by other songwriters (in this case John D. Loudermilk). "Twenty Flight Rock" was written by AMI staff writer Ned Fairchild (a pen name, her real name is Nelda Fairchild). AMI granted Cochran a co-writer credit but no royalties, a common arrangement by which publishers move songs from demos to commercial recordings. This allowed Cochran to rewrite or add to the song to turn it into a rock and roll song. Fairchild, who was not a rock and roll performer, merely provided the initial form of the song, and the co-writing credit reflects Cochran's changes and contributions to the final product.

In November 1957 Liberty Records released Cochran's only album released during his lifetime, *Singin' to My Baby*. The album included Eddie's first hit "Sittin' in the Balcony". There were only a few rockers on this album, and Liberty seemed to want to move Cochran more into the pop music direction. In 1958 however Cochran seemed to find his stride in the famous teenage anthem "Summertime Blues" (co-written with Jerry Capehart). With this song Cochran was established as an important influence on music in the late 1950s, both lyrically and musically. The song, released on Liberty recording No. 55144, charted at No. 8 on August 25, 1958. Cochran's brief career included only a few more hits, such as "C'mon Everybody", "Somethin' Else", "Teenage

Heaven", and his posthumous UK number one hit "Three Steps to Heaven." Eddie Cochran remained popular in the UK throughout the 1960s and scored more posthumous hits such as "My Way", "Weekend" and "Nervous Breakdown".

Eddie Cochran was also a prolific studio musician and backed many artists playing lead guitar. In 1959 he played lead for Skeets McDonald at Columbia's studios for "You Oughta See Grandma Rock" and "Heart Breaking Mama". In a session for Gene Vincent in march 1958 he contributed his trademark low bass voice as heard on Summertime Blues. The recordings were issued on the album *A Gene Vincent Record Date*.

In early 1959, two of Cochran's friends, Buddy Holly and Ritchie Valens, along with the Big Bopper, were killed in a plane crash while on tour. Eddie's friends and family later said that he was badly shaken by their deaths, and he developed a morbid premonition that he would also die young. He was anxious to give up life on the road and spend his time in the studio making music, thereby reducing the chance of suffering a similar fatal accident while touring. However, financial responsibilities required that he continue to perform live, and that led to his acceptance of an offer to tour the United Kingdom in 1960.

UK tour and death

Memorial plaque at Rowden Hill, Chippenham

On Saturday, April 16, 1960, at about 11.50 p.m., while on tour in the United Kingdom, 21-year-old Cochran died as a result of a traffic accident in a taxi (a Ford Consul, not, as widely reported, a London hackney carriage) traveling through Chippenham, Wiltshire, on the A4. The speeding taxi blew a tire, lost control, and crashed into a lamp post on Rowden Hill, where a plaque now marks the spot (no other car was involved). Cochran, who was seated in the centre of the back seat, threw himself over his fiancée Sharon Sheeley to shield her, and was thrown out of the car when the door flew open. He was taken to St. Martin's Hospital, Bath, where he died at 4:10 p.m. the following day of severe head injuries. Cochran's body was flown home and his remains were buried on April 25, 1960, at Forest Lawn Memorial Park in Cypress, California.

Songwriter Sharon Sheeley and singer Gene Vincent survived the crash, Vincent sustaining lasting injuries to an already permanently damaged leg that would shorten his career and affect him for the rest of his life. The taxi driver, George Martin, was convicted of dangerous driving, fined £50, disqualified from driving for 15 years, and sentenced to prison for six months (although by some accounts he served no prison time at all). His driving privileges were reinstated by the court in 1969. The car and other items from the crash were impounded at the local police station until a coroner's inquest could be held. David Harman, a police cadet at the station who would later become known as Dave Dee of the band Dave Dee, Dozy, Beaky, Mick & Tich, taught himself to play guitar on Cochran's impounded Gretsch. Earlier in the tour, the same guitar had been carried to the car for Cochran by a young fan, Mark Feld, who would later be known as Marc Bolan of T. Rex and would also die in a car crash. A posthumous album, *My Way*, was released in 1964.

A memorial stone to commemorate Eddie Cochran can be found in the grounds of St Martin's Hospital in Bath. The stone was restored in 2010 (on the 50th anniversary of his death) and can be found in the old chapel grounds at St Martin's Hospital. A memorial plaque can also be found next to the sundial at the back of the old chapel.

Posthumous releases and honors

Cochran was a prolific performer, and the British label Rockstar Records has released more of his music posthumously than had been released during his life. The company is still looking for unpublished songs.

One of his posthumous releases was "Three Stars," a tribute to J.P. Richardson, better known as The Big Bopper, and Eddie's friends Buddy Holly and Ritchie Valens, who had all died together in a plane crash just one year earlier. It was originally written and recorded by Tommy Dee just hours after the deaths were officially reported, and Cochran recorded his version the day after. His voice broke during the lyrics about Valens and Holly.

In 1987, Cochran was inducted into the Rock and Roll Hall of Fame. His pioneering contribution to the genre of rockabilly has also been recognized by the Rockabilly Hall of Fame. Several of his songs have been rereleased since his death, such as "C'mon Everybody," which was a number 14 hit in 1983 in the UK. *Rolling Stone* ranked him number 84 on their 2003 list of the 100 greatest guitarists of all time.

Cochran's life is chronicled in several publications, including *Don't Forget Me—The Eddie Cochran Story*, written by Julie Mundy and Darrel Higham ISBN 0-8230-7931-7), and *Three Steps to Heaven*, written by Bobby Cochran ISBN 0-634-03252-6).

On June 2, 2008, *The Very Best of Eddie Cochran* was released by EMI Records.

Influence

One of the first rock and roll artists to write his own songs and overdub tracks, Cochran is credited also with being one of the first to use an unwound third string in order to "bend' notes up a whole tone—an innovation (imparted to UK guitarist Joe Brown, who secured much session work as a result) that has since become an essential part of the standard rock guitar vocabulary. Artists such as The Rolling Stones, Bruce Springsteen, Van Halen, Tom Petty,

Rod Stewart, Motörhead, Humble Pie, Commander Cody and His Lost Planet Airmen, Lemmy Kilmister, The Head Cat, The Damned, UFO (band), T. Rex, Stray Cats, Brian Setzer, Cliff Richard, The Who, The Beach Boys, The Beatles, Blue Cheer, Led Zeppelin, The White Stripes, The Sex Pistols, Rush, Buck Owens, Tiger Army, Dion, Simple Minds, Guitar Wolf, Paul McCartney, Alan Jackson, Keith Richards & The X-Pensive Winos, and Jimi Hendrix have covered his songs.

It was because Paul McCartney knew the chords and words to "Twenty Flight Rock" that he became a member of The Beatles. John Lennon was so impressed that he invited Paul to play with his band The Quarrymen. Jimi Hendrix performed "Summertime Blues" early in his career, and Pete Townshend of The Who was heavily influenced by Cochran's guitar style ("Summertime Blues" was a Who live staple at one time and is featured on their *Live at Leeds* album). Glam rock artist Marc Bolan had his main Les Paul model refinished in a transparent orange to resemble the Gretsch 6120 guitar played by Cochran, who was his music hero. He was also a heavy influence on the nascent rockabilly guitar legend Brian Setzer from Stray Cats, who plays a 6120 almost like Cochran, whom he portrayed in the film *La Bamba*. Cochran is easily one of the first musicians, alongside Chuck Berry, whom the late Rory Gallagher was always quick to mention as a strong influence on his musical taste and performance.

In 1988 "C'mon Everybody" was used by Levi Strauss & Co. in an advertisement to promote its 501 Jeans catalogue and rereleased as a promotional single, hitting No. 14 in the UK charts. The advertisement told a story of how the narrator, Sharon Sheeley, attracted Cochran by wearing her 501s.

Guitars

When playing with Hank Cochran, Eddie Cochran played a Gibson L-4C archtop acoustic guitar with a florentine cutaway and a DeArmond 'Rhythm Chief' pickup, which can be clearly seen in the Cochran Brothers publicity photograph.

Later, Cochran moved to a 1955 Gretsch 6120 Chet Atkins G-brand Western model, which Eddie had modified. He replaced the neck position De Armond Dynasonic pickup with a black covered Gibson P-90 pickup. He also used Martin acoustic guitars.

Discography

Chart positions are from the Billboard Hot 100.

U.S. Singles

"Skinny Jim" b/w "Half Loved" (July 1956)
"Sittin' in the Balcony" b/w "Dark Lonely Street" (February 1957) Chart no. 18
"One Kiss" b/w "Mean When I'm Mad" (May 1957)
"Drive in Show" b/w "Am I Blue" Liberty F55087 (July 1957) Chart no. 82
"Twenty Flight Rock" b/w "Cradle baby" (November 1957)
"Jeannie Jeannie Jeannie" b/w "Pocketful of Hearts" (January 1958) Chart no. 94
"Teresa" b/w "Pretty Girl" (May 1958)
"Summertime Blues" b/w "Love Again" Liberty F55144 (July 1958) Chart no. 8
"C'mon Everybody" b/w "Don't Ever Let Me Go" Liberty F55166 (October 1958) Chart no. 35
"Teenage Heaven" b/w "I Remember" Liberty 55177 (February 1959) Chart no. 99
"Somethin' Else" b/w "Boll Weevil Song" Liberty 55203 (July 1959) Chart no. 58
"Hallelujah I Love Her So" b/w "Cradle Baby" (November 1959)
"Cut Across Shorty" b/w "Three Steps To Heaven" (March 1960)
"Lonely" b/w "Sweetie Pie" (August 1960)
"Lonely" b/w "Weekend" (December 1961)
Source http://en.wikipedia.org/wiki/Eddie_Cochran

Ervin Williams

Ervin L. "Wee Willie" Williams (December 18, 1935 - August 28, 1999) was an American rockabilly pioneer musician.

Nicknamed "Wee Willie" as well as "Early," Williams was born in Millinocket, Maine where began playing guitar as a boy. In his teens he became part of The Northern Lights, a band that toured his native Maine and across the nearby border in New Brunswick, Canada. He eventually made his way to Virginia where he became Gene Vincent's first rhythm guitarist as part of "The Blue Caps." When Vincent was signed by Capitol Records, Wee Willie Williams participated in the creation of classic recordings such as 1956's "Be Bop-A-Lula" and "Race with the Devil."

For his pioneering role in the genre, Williams has been recognized by the Rock and Roll Hall of Fame and the Rockabilly Hall of Fame. Williams died as the result of an accidental gunshot injury in Bradenton, Florida in August, 1999.
Source http://en.wikipedia.org/wiki/Ervin_Williams

Gene Summers

Gene Summers			
Born	January 3, 1939	(age 73) Dallas, Texas, U.S.	
		Genres	Rock and roll, Rockabilly

Occupations	Singer, songwriter, publisher, record producer
Instruments	Vocals, guitar
Years active	1958-present
Labels	Mercury Records Jan/Jane Records Jamie Records Tear Drop Records Capri Records Rhino/Atlantic Records Warner Music Group artists Jubilee Records Apex Records (Canada) W&G Records/Australia Alta Records Charay Records, Collectables Records EMI/Big Beat Norton Records Charly Records Various Indie Labels
Associated acts	The Rebels, The Tom Toms, Bill Smith Combo
Website	Gene Summers Rockabilly Hall of Fame Page

Gene Summers (born January 3, 1939 in Dallas, Texas) is an American rock/rockabilly singer and entertainer. Some of his classic recordings include "School of Rock 'n Roll", "Straight Skirt", "Nervous", "Gotta Lotta That", "Twixteen", "Alabama Shake" and his biggest-selling single "Big Blue Diamonds". Summers was inducted into the Rockabilly Hall of Fame in 1997 and The Southern Legends Entertainment & Performing Arts Hall of Fame in 2005. He still performs worldwide and celebrated his 50th anniversary as a recording artist in 2008 with the release of *Reminisce Cafe*.

Summers graduated from Duncanville High School in 1957 and attended Arlington State College, now known as the University of Texas at Arlington. That same year, he formed the rockabilly band The Rebels and performed on *Joe Bill's Country Picnic* on KRLD-TV where they were spotted by songwriter Jed Tarver. This led to the band being signed by newly-found Jan Records. Their first record was released on February 1, 1958, under the name of Gene Summers & His Rebels.

Partial discography

Rock 'n Roll Volume 2. 1973, Holland
The Southern Cat Rocks On 1975, Switzerland
Mister Rock and Roll 1977, Switzerland
Rock a Boogie Shake 1980, Sweden
Early Rocking Recordings 1981, Holland
Texas Rock and Roll 1981, France
Gene Summers in Nashville 1981, France
Dance Dance Dance 1981, UK
Rock 'n Roll Tour - "Live" In Scandinavia 1983, Sweden
School Of Rock 'n Roll (album) 1994, Holland
Sounds Like Elvis CD 1996 (compilation), USA
The Ultimate School of Rock & Roll 1997, USA
Rockaboogie Shake 1999, UK
Do Right Daddy 2004, Sweden
Reminisce Cafe 2008, USA
Taboo! 2011, USA

Television, Films and DVDs

(incomplete)
Hi-School High Lites Show - Dallas, TX 1956
The Neal Jones Show - Dallas, TX 1956
Joe Bill's Country Picnic - Dallas, TX 1957-'58
Jerry Haynes' "Top Ten Dance Party" - Dallas, TX 1958
The Larry Kane Show - Houston, TX 1958
The Ted Steele Bandstand Show - New York City-1958
The Milt Grant Show- Washington, DC 1958
The Buddy Deane Show - Baltimore, MD 1958
The Larry Kane Show - Houston, TX 1964
Hi-Ho Shebang Show - Ft. Worth, TX 1965-'66
Le Grand Échiquier - Paris, France 1981
World Class Championship Wrestling - Dallas, TX 1981 *(see Ring announcers)*
Warner-Amex Special *Gene Summers 'Live At Zebo's* - 1983
Backlot (movie-short) - 1986
No Safe Haven (movie) - 1989
Rob's Chop Shop (TV Pilot) - 1996
Billy Martin (movie) - 2000
Big Beat Generation Vol. 1 (DVD) - 2009 (Big Beat Records, France)
Big Beat Story Vol. 2 (DVD) - 2011 (Big Beat Records, France)

Cover versions of Gene Summers songs

Many songs popularized by Gene Summers have been recorded by other artists. Cover versions include:
Alabama Shake - by Crazy Cavan and the Rhythm Rockers (1976), The Flying Saucers (1976), C.S.A (1978), Teddy and The Tigers (1979), The Rockabilly Rebs (1979), Rockin' Lord Lee & The Outlaws (1988), Tony Vincent (1993), Badland Slingers (1999), The Shaking Silouets (1999), The TTs (2002), Rawhide (2004), King Drapes (2003), Hurricains (2007) *("live" video)*, The Muskrats (2009), *("live" video)*, Deke Dickerson (2010) *("live" video)*,
Almost 12 O'Clock - by Rock-Ola (1981),
Big Blue Diamonds - by Jacky Ward (1971), Ernest Tubb (1972), Mel Street (1972), Jerry Lee Lewis (1973), Bobby Crown (1980), Dan Walser (1996), Dennis Gilley (2000), Lembo Allen (2004) Rance Norton (2008), Back In Time Band (2009) *("live" video)*,
The Clown - by J. Frank Wilson (1959),
Crazy Cat Corner - by Bill Peck (1998) *(re-written vocal adaptation titled 'The Night Elvis Missed The Boat")*,
Fancy Dan - by Darrel Higham (1998), The Rocking Boys (2003), Eddie & The Flatheads (2003), Houserockers (2005), Roughcuts (????), John Lewis Trio (2010) *("live" video)*,
Gotta Lotta That - by Johnny Devlin (1958), Andy Lee & Tennessee Rain (2000), Rudy LaCrioux and the All-Stars (2001)
I'll Never Be Lonely - by Eddie Clendening (2006)
My Picture - by The Sprites (Original

Drifters) (1962)
Nervous - by Johnny Devlin (1959), Robert Gordon *with* Link Wray (1979), Lonestars (1981), Rock-Ola & The Freewheelers (2000), T-Bird Gang (2009). **NOTE:** *Gene Vincent attempted twice to record a demo of "Nervous" in home recordings in Dallas in 1957 which were released in 1998 on Dragon Street Records CD "The Lost Dallas Sessions"*
Reminisce Cafe - by Pete Moss (2004) *(Taped during a "live" broadcast on The Pete Moss Show on KDWN-AM Radio, Las Vegas, Nevada)*
Rockaboogie Shake - by Lennerockers (2002)
School Of Rock 'n Roll - by Savage Kalman and The Explosion Rockets (1979), The Polecats (1980), Red Hot Max And The Cats (1989), The Rhythm Rockets (1989), Johnny Reno (1990), The Lennerockers (1991), The Alphabets (1991), Mess Of Booze (1993), The Vees (1995), The Blue Moon Rockers (1996), The Cornell Hurd Band (2002), Thierry LeCoz (2003), Rockin' Ryan and The Real Goners (2003), Lucky Strike Band (2003), Los Aceleradores (2004) *("live" video)*, Alan Leatherwood (2004), The Starlight Wranglers (2004), The Greyhounds (2004), Black Knights (2004), Rory Justice (2004), Big Sandy & his Fly-Rite Boys (2005) *("live" video)*, Mike Mok and The Em-Tones (2007) *("live" video)*, Bob Glazebrook & Houserockers (2009) *("live" video)*, Dixie Stompers (2009) *("live" video)*, The Muskrats (2009) *("live" video)*, Black Knights (2010), The Jets & Lights Out (2010) *("live" video)*, The Bop A Tones (2010) *("live" video)*, Gene Vincent - UNISSUED private recording, (late 1960s). *According to a 1998 Now Dig This! magazine review of Derek Henderson's book "Gene Vincent A Discography", there's a complete A-Z listing of the 217 song titles that he's (Vincent) known to have recorded- everything from the Capitol biggies such as "Say Mama", Rocky Road Blues" and "Wildcat" to lesser known items such as private recordings of "Stand By Me", "Chain Gang" and "School Of Rock 'n Roll".*
She Bops A Lot - by The Lightcrust Doughboys (2000)
Straight Skirt - by The Diamonds (1958), Johnny Devlin (1958), Ronnie Dawson (1958), The Sureshots (2005)
Turnip Greens - by Darrel Higham & The Enforcers (1992)
Twixteen - by Teddy and The Tigers (1979), Runnin' Wild (1997), Jimmy Velvit (2000) *(The Velvit version is a rewritten vocal adaptation titled "Waiting For Elvis")*
You Said You Loved Me - by Sid and Billy King (1988)
Source http://en.wikipedia.org/wiki/Gene_Summers

Glen Glenn (singer)

Orin Glenn Troutman (born October 24, 1934), known professionally as **Glen Glenn**, is an American rockabilly singer whose career began in the early 1950s and continues to this day.

He was born in Joplin, Missouri. In late 1957, he signed with Era Records in Los Angeles, California and in January 1958 his first single was released, "Everybody's Movin'" backed with "I'm Glad My Baby's Gone".

Source http://en.wikipedia.org/wiki/Glen_Glenn_(singer)

James Burton

James Burton

James Burton Live in Concert - 2009
Background information
Born	21 August 1939 Dubberly, Louisiana United States
Genres	Rock and roll, rockabilly, country, country rock
Occupations	Musician
Instruments	Guitar, dobro
Years active	1952–present
Associated acts	TCB Band, Elvis Presley, Ricky Nelson, Emmylou Harris, John Denver
Website	www.james-burton.net

Notable instruments
1953 Fender Telecaster
1969 Paisley Red Fender Telecaster

James Burton (born August 21, 1939, in Dubberly, Louisiana) is an American guitarist. A member of the Rock and Roll Hall of Fame since 2001 (his induction speech was given by longtime fan Keith Richards), Burton has also been recognized by the Rockabilly Hall of Fame. Critic Mark Demming writes that "Burton has a well-deserved reputation as one of the finest guitar pickers in either country or rock ... [Burton is] one of the best guitar players to ever touch a fretboard."

James Burton is also known as the "Master of the (Fender) Telecaster."

Since the 1950s, Burton has recorded and performed with an array of notable singers, including Bob Luman, Dale Hawkins, Ricky Nelson, Elvis Presley, Johnny Cash, Merle Haggard, Glen Campbell, John Denver, Gram Parsons, Emmylou Harris, Jerry Lee Lewis, Claude King, Elvis Costello, Joe Osborn, Roy Orbison, Joni Mitchell, Vince Gill, Suzi Quatro and Allen "Puddler" Harris.

Biography

Early life and career

Burton was born in Dubberly in south Webster Parish near Minden, Louisiana, to Guy M. Burton (1909–2001) and the former Lola Poland (1914–2011), a native of rural Fryeburg in Bienville Parish. She was the daughter of James and Althius Poland. Burton's wife is Louise Burton.

Self-taught, Burton began playing guitar in childhood. By the time he was thirteen, he was playing semi-professionally. A year later he was hired to be part of the staff band for the popular *Louisiana Hayride* radio show in Shreveport. While he was still a teenager, Burton left Shreveport for Los Angeles, where he joined Ricky Nelson's band. There, he made numerous recordings as a session musician. Burton created and played the guitar solo on Dale Hawkins 1957 hit song "Susie Q", a record that would become one of the Rock and Roll Hall of Fame's 500 Songs that Shaped Rock and Roll.

With Rick Nelson

Burton played lead guitar on all of Rick Nelson's recordings between 1958 and 1967. In 1965 he started working on the television program *Shindig!* and eventually left Nelson's band two years later. The television exposure led to continuous recording session work with a huge variety of artists, mostly as an unattributed sideman. Due to the volume of work, Burton turned down an offer to join Bob Dylan's first touring band, and another offer to play on Elvis Presley's 1968 comeback TV special *Elvis*.

With Elvis Presley

In 1969, Presley again asked Burton to join his show in Las Vegas, and this time Burton agreed. Burton formed the TCB Band and backed Presley from 1969 until Presley's death in 1977. A hallmark of Elvis' live shows in this period was his exhortation, "Play it, James," as a cue for the guitarist's solos. For the first season in Vegas 1969 Burton played his red standard telecaster. He shortly after purchased the now familiar pink paisley custom telecaster. Burton was not sure that Elvis would like it - but since he did, James used it in every show.

Since 1998, Burton has played lead guitar in *Elvis: The Concert* which reunited some of Elvis' former TCB bandmates, background singers and Elvis' orchestral conductor (mostly from the "concert years" 1969-1977) live on stage.

With John Denver

During 1975 and 1976, while still touring with Presley, Burton was one of the first members to join and tour with Emmylou Harris as part of her backing band, the "Hot Band", after the death of Gram Parsons. He was joined by a cast of talented musicians which included his bandmate with Presley, Glen D. Hardin, and newer musicians which included Rodney Crowell. However, once Presley was ready to return to the road, Burton returned to perform with him, although the others, including Hardin, elected to continue with Harris. Just before Presley died in 1977, Burton was called to play on a John Denver television special. During the taping, Denver asked if Burton would consider going on a European tour. Burton said he was working with Elvis, but if scheduling permitted, he would be glad to go. Shortly after Elvis' death, Burton began a regular collaboration with Denver. The first album they recorded was *I Want to Live*.

During the sessions, Burton and Denver talked about a band. Glen Hardin and Jerry Scheff, from Presley's band, joined the new band too. Burton remained a member of Denver's band until 1994, but often toured in parallel with other artists including Jerry Lee Lewis. In the 16 years Burton worked with Denver, they recorded 12 albums and toured around the world. While touring with Denver, Burton carried several instruments, including backup Dobros and a spare 1969 Pink Paisley Fender Telecaster he had used as a touring guitarist with Elvis Presley during the 1970s. He rejoined Denver in 1995 for the Wildlife Concert. When Denver died in 1997, Burton spoke at his memorial service in Aspen, Colorado.

Recent career

Statue of Burton at the Shreveport Municipal Auditorium

Burton's later career included work with Ricky Nelson, Elvis Presley, John Denver, Merle Haggard, Gram Parsons, Rodney Crowell and Emmylou Harris. Beginning with *King of America* (1986), Burton recorded and toured with Elvis Costello intermittently for about a decade. In 1988, he was a prominent part of the acclaimed Cinemax special, *Roy Orbison and Friends, A Black and White Night*. In 1990, Burton moved back to his hometown of Shreveport permanently.

In the fall of 2004, Burton recorded *Matt Lucas-Back in the Saddle Again*, a sequel to the Matt Lucas album *The Chicago Sessions*. The album features rockabilly and country music, and was released in May 2006 by Ten O Nine Records.

In 2005, Burton started the annual James Burton International Guitar Festival to raise money for his charitable foundation. The festival is held in the Red River District of Shreveport.

In 2007 he was inducted into the Musicians Hall of Fame in Nashville as a member of the L.A. session player group known as The Wrecking Crew. In 2008, Burton was asked by Brad Paisley to play on his upcoming album *Play*. Burton went along for the ride and played on an instrumental track called "Cluster Pluck," as did Vince Gill, Steve Wariner, Redd Volkaert, Albert Lee, John Jorgenson, and Brent Mason. At the 51st Grammy Awards in 2009 the song won Best Country Instrumental Performance.

On August 22, 2009, on stage at his

James Burton International Guitar Festival, James Burton was inducted into The Louisiana Music Hall of Fame.

On July 15, 2010 Rolling Stone Magazine announced Eric Clapton and James Burton will provide backup guitars on the track "You Can Have Her." for the new Jerry Lee Lewis album Mean Old Man, scheduled for release the fall of 2010.

On June 9, 2012, Burton appeared in the Shreveport Auditorium for a presentation of Garrison Keillor's *Prairie Home Companion*.

Equipment

Burton works with a variety of amplifiers to provide flexibility and a wide range of sounds. He has used a Music Man 210-150, an old Fender Twin with K model Lansing speakers, and a 1964 Fender Deluxe. His primary guitar has always been a Fender Telecaster, beginning with an early blonde model his parents bought for him around 1951 or 1952. His 1969 Paisley Red (better known as Pink Paisley) Telecaster became the basis for a Fender Artist Signature model in 1991, with Lace Sensor pickups and a TBX tone circuit. Five years later his 1953 Candy Apple Red Telecaster was the inspiration for a standard version Artist Signature model featuring two Fender Texas Special Tele single coil pickups and a vintage-style 6-saddle bridge. In 2006, the Signature Paisley model was redesigned with a red paisley flame design over a black body, plus three specially designed blade pickups, a no-load tone control and S-1 switching system.

Source http://en.wikipedia.org/wiki/James_Burton

Jesse Dayton

For the 19th-century New York politician, see Jesse C. Dayton.

Jesse Dayton is an Austin, Texas-based honky tonk and rockabilly artist best known for his guitar contributions to albums by country legends including Johnny Cash, Waylon Jennings, and Willie Nelson. He is also notable for his collaborations with horror film director Rob Zombie who has commissioned Dayton on multiple occasions to record music to accompany his films.

Dayton was born in Beaumont, Texas where he was raised on the music of George Jones, Hank Williams, and Lefty Frizzell, all the while harboring an affinity for the spirit of punk with bands like the Clash. After touring with two rockabilly bands, the Road Kings and the Alamo Jets, Dayton ventured off into solo territory, recording his Americana-chart-topping record *Raisin' Cain*.

Since then Dayton has released several different solo albums and worked with a variety of country rock artists, most notably Waylon Jennings and Johnny Cash on Right For The Time after Jennings injured his picking thumb and required a guitar stand-in. Dayton also contributed guitarwork on albums by the Supersuckers and Kris Kristofferson.

In 2004, horror film director Rob Zombie commissioned Jesse Dayton to record an album for the fictional characters Banjo & Sullivan from his sophomore feature *The Devil's Rejects*. The resulting album was a collection of tongue-in-cheek honkey-tonk country entitled *Banjo & Sullivan: The Ultimate Collection*. In Zombie's *Halloween II*, Dayton performs as the lead singer and guitarist of the fictional psychobilly band Captain Clegg & the Night Creatures. He is slated to release an album entitled *Rob Zombie presents Captain Clegg & The Night Creatures (music from Halloween II)* on August 28, same day as the film *Halloween II* is set to premiere.

Source http://en.wikipedia.org/wiki/Jesse_Dayton

Johnny Carroll

Johnny Carroll

Background information

Birth name	John Lewis Carrell
Born	October 23, 1937 Cleburne, Texas
Origin	Godley, Texas
Died	February 18, 1995 (aged Dallas, Texas
Genres	Rock and Roll
Occupations	Singer, Guitarist
Years active	1956 - 1985
Labels	Decca Records, Sun Rec Warner Bros. Records

Notable instruments

Guitar

Johnny Carroll (October 23, 1937 – February 18, 1995) was an American rockabilly musician.

Biography

Born John Lewis Carrell (Carrell was printed incorrectly as Carroll on the record label), Carroll began recording for Decca Records in the middle of the 1950s. He released several singles, but none of them saw significant success, though they are now critically acclaimed. His records were eclipsed by the success of other rockabilly and early rock & roll musicians such as Elvis Presley, Jerry Lee Lewis, and Johnny Cash.

His career ended toward the end of the 1950s, but he made a comeback in 1974 with a Gene Vincent tribute song. He continued to record well into the 1980s. For many years he was connected with the Cellar Club in Ft Worth, Texas and other Cellar Clubs around Texas. He died of liver failure on January 13, 1995, and is buried in his hometown of Godley, Texas. In 1996 a 33-track reissue of his early recordings was released as *Rock Baby Rock It: 1955-1960*.

Discography

Early recordings

Year	Title	Record label
1956	Rock'n'Roll Ruby / Trying To Get To You	Decca Records
1956	Wild Wild Women / Corrine, Corrine	Decca Records
1956	Hot Rock / Crazy Crazy Lovin'	Decca Records
1957	That's The Way I Love / I'll Wait	Phillips International
1959	The Swing / Bandstand Doll	Warner Bros. Records
1959	Sugar / Lost Lost Without You	
1960	Run Come See / Trudy	WA Records
1962	Run Come See / The Sally Ann	Duchess Records
1956	**EP** Hot Rock Corrine, Corrine Crazy Crazy Lovin' Wild Wild Women Crazy Little Mama Cut Out Hearts Of Stone Love Is A Merry-Go-Round Sexy Ways Stingy Thing Why Cry Be-Bop-A-Lula Is Back On The Scene Cat With The Skin Lonesome Boy Sugar Lips	Decca Records not released

Later recordings

"Gene Vincent Rock" (or "The Black Leather Rebel") (1974)
"Rock, Baby, Rock It" (Sun Records, 1975)
Texabilly (1977)
Screamin' Demon Heatwave (Seville Records, 1983)
Crazy Hot Rock (Charly Records, 1985)
Shades of Vincent (with Judy Lindsey) (Charly Records)
Source http://en.wikipedia.org/wiki/Johnny_Carroll

Luther Perkins

Luther Perkins

Birth name	Luther Monroe Perkins
Born	January 8, 1928 Memphis, Tennessee
Died	August 5, 1968 (aged 40) Nashville, Tennessee
Genres	Country, rockabilly
Occupations	Musician
Instruments	Electric Guitar
Years active	1954–1968
Associated acts	Johnny Cash, Tennessee Three

Notable instruments

Fender Esquire, Fender Jazzmaster, Fender Jaguar

Luther Monroe Perkins (January 8, 1928 – August 5, 1968) was an American country music guitarist and a member of the Tennessee Three, the backup band for singer Johnny Cash. Perkins was an iconic figure in what would become known as rockabilly music. His creatively simple, sparsely-embellished, rhythmic use of Fender Esquire,

Jazzmaster and Jaguar guitars is credited for creating Cash's signature "boom-chicka-boom" style.

Early life and musical beginnings

Perkins was born in Memphis, Tennessee, the son of a Baptist preacher. He grew up in Como, Mississippi, and taught himself to play rhythm guitar.

Perkins started his career in 1953 as a mechanic at Automobile Sales Company in Memphis. He specialized in electrical systems and radio repairs. Roy Cash, Sr., older brother of Johnny Cash, was service manager at the dealership. At the time, the younger Cash was stationed in Germany with the US Air Force. At Automobile Sales, Perkins met co-workers Marshall Grant and A. W. 'Red' Kernodle. Grant, Kernodle and Perkins began bringing their guitars to work, and would play together when repair business was slow.

When Johnny Cash moved to Memphis after returning from Germany in 1954, Ray Cash introduced him to Grant, Kernodle and Perkins. The four began to get together in the evenings at Perkins's or Grant's home and play songs. It was during this time that they decided to form a band, with Grant acquiring a string bass, Kernodle a six-string steel guitar, and Perkins buying a somewhat-abused Fender Esquire electric guitar from the O.K. Houck Piano Co. in Memphis. The guitar had been modified by a previous owner, and the volume and tone controls were dysfunctional.

"Boom-chicka-boom" style

Since he could not control the volume of the single-pickup instrument, Perkins began the practice of muting the three bass strings (E, A and D) with the heel of his right hand, much in the style of Merle Travis, and scratching a rhythm pattern (as heard on Sun Records recordings prior to 1958). This pattern developed into a more defined, varying 1/8-8/5/8-8 picking (with random syncopation) on later Sun recordings and for the rest of Perkins' career.

In late 1954, when Cash got an audition with producer Sam Phillips at Sun Records, he brought Perkins, Grant and Kernodle along to back him instrumentally. The experience made Kernodle nervous, and he ended up leaving before the session was over, with Perkins and Grant providing the instrumentation.

Perkins, as a member of the Tennessee Two (later, the Tennessee Three, with the addition of drummer W.S. "Fluke" Holland), toured with Cash and appeared on most of his recordings. He was well known for his laconic, focused demeanor on stage. He was often the target of jokes by Cash, who would make comments such as "Luther's been dead for years, but he just doesn't know it".

Personal

Perkins was married twice. He and his first wife, Bertie, separated while they were living in southern California in 1959. Perkins had three daughters from this marriage: Linda, Vicki and Claudia. He later married Margie Higgins; they had one daughter, Kathy. Margie Perkins Beaver still appears at Johnny Cash reunion events.

His hobbies were knitting, fishing and guitar. Examples of his knitting are on display at the Musicians Hall of Fame and Museum in Nashville, Tennessee.

He was a close friend of singer-songwriter Kris Kristofferson. At the time of his death, he was planning to open his own music publishing company and give Kristofferson his first break.

Perkins' younger brother, Thomas, was a successful rock 'n' roll singer in the 1950s and 1960s, under the name of Thomas Wayne.

In his autobiography, Johnny Cash wrote that Perkins was mildly addicted to amphetamines. They started taking drugs together in the late 1950s.

Perkin's nickname was "L.M", the initials of his first and second name "Luther Monroe". Singer-guitarist Carl Perkins, who was also a member of Cash's touring show, was not related to Luther Perkins.

Death

During the early morning hours of August 3, 1968, Perkins returned from fishing on Old Hickory Lake to his newly-constructed home on Riverwood Drive in Hendersonville, Tennessee. He apparently went to sleep in the living room while holding a lit cigarette. His daughter awoke around 6:00 am to find the living room in flames and Perkins collapsed near the door. An emergency crew rushed Perkins to Vanderbilt University Hospital, where he was kept in intensive care until finally succumbing on Monday, August 5, 1968.

His grave is near the graves of Johnny Cash and June Carter Cash at Hendersonville Memorial Park in Hendersonville, Tennessee.

Luther Perkins was inducted into the Rockabilly Hall of Fame. Perkins and Marshall Grant, as The Tennessee Two, were inducted into the Musicians Hall of Fame.

In 1980, Perkins's daughters from his first marriage filed suit against Johnny Cash for embezzling funds that were to have provided retirement income for Perkins. This lawsuit was filed coincidentally with actions taken by the other founding Tennessee Three member, Marshall Grant, against Cash for wrongfully firing Grant and embezzlement of Grant's retirement funds. Both lawsuits were eventually settled out-of-court.

Walk the Line

In *Walk The Line*, the 2005 biopic of Johnny Cash, Perkins is portrayed by Dan John Miller. Perkins's future death is alluded to in the film in a bus scene where Cash (played by Joaquin Phoenix) walks past a sleeping Perkins. Perkins is depicted as asleep with his cigarette still burning in his mouth. Cash stubs it out in the ashtray in front of him which references Perkins's eventual death.

Source http://en.wikipedia.org/wiki/Luther_Perkins

Rocky Burnette

Rocky Burnette
Birth name Jonathan Burnette
Born Memphis, Tennessee, United States
Origin Memphis, Tennessee, United States
Genres Rock and roll, rockabilly
Occupations Singer, Guitarist
Instruments Singing, Guitar
Years active 1979–present
Labels EMI America

Rocky Burnette (born **Jonathan Burnette**, 12 June 1953) is an American rock and roll singer/musician and the son of rock and roll pioneer, Johnny Burnette. He is best known for his 1980 hit single "Tired of Toein' the Line."

Career

Rocky Burnette was born in Memphis, Tennessee, and became part of the early 1980s revival of the rockabilly style. He released his first album, *Son of Rock 'n' Roll*, on EMI America in 1979. In the summer of 1980, his single "Tired of Toein' the Line" became a Top Ten hit in the United States. The song was also popular internationally, becoming a No. 1 hit in Australia and peaking at No. 3 in South Africa. It reached No. 58 in the UK Singles Chart. EMI America's financial problems interfered with promotion efforts for the follow-up singles (several of which became hits in other countries), and Burnette's second album, *Heart Stopper*, was not successful.

In 1981, Burnette toured Europe with the final version of his late father's The Rock and Roll Trio. He also used the band on his next album, *Get Hot or Go Home!* on Enigma Records. It also sold poorly, and Enigma dropped Burnette and the Trio rather than release a follow-up.

Burnette worked with Rosie Flores and Dwight Twilley in the mid-1990s, and also contributed vocals and the original "Trouble Is I'm in Love With You" to Paul Burlison's 1997 *Train Kept A-Rollin'*. In 1996, Burnette released *Tear It Up* on Core Records.

Burnette wrote the European hit "You Got Away With Love" for Percy Sledge in 1997. He continues to tour internationally and maintains a devoted fan base in the US.

Source http://en.wikipedia.org/wiki/Rocky_Burnette

Rosie Flores

Rosie Flores
Born September 10, 1950
Origin San Antonio, Texas
Genres Country
Occupations Singer
Instruments Vocals, Guitar
Years active 1968–present
Labels Reprise
HighTone
Rounder
Watermelon
Eminent
Durango Rose
Emergent
Bloodshot Records
Associated acts Rosie and the Screamers
Asleep at the Wheel
Website Official Site

Rosie Flores (born September 10, 1950 in San Antonio, Texas) is a rockabilly and country music artist of Mexican American heritage. Her music blends rockabilly, honky tonk, jazz, and Western swing along with traditional influences from her Tex-Mex heritage. She currently resides in Austin, Texas, where August 31 was declared Rosie Flores Day by the Austin City Council in 2006.

In 1995, she joined Wanda Jackson on a coast-to-coast North American tour.

She has appeared on *Austin City Limits* and *Late Night with Conan O'Brien*.

Discography

Albums

Year	Album	US Country	Label
1987	Rosie Flores	67	Reprise
1989	After the Farm		HighTone
1993	Once More with Feeling		
1995	Rockabilly Filly		
1996	Honky Tonk Reprise		Rounder
1997	A Little Bit of Heartache		Watermelon
1999	Dance Hall Dreams		Rounder
2001	Speed of Sound		Eminent
2004	Bandera Highway Single Rose		HighTone Durango Rose
2005	Christmasville		Emergent
2009	Girl of the Century (with The Pine Valley Cosmonauts)		Bloodshot

Singles

Year	Single	US Country	Album
1986	"I'm Walkin'"		single only
1987	"Crying Over You"	51	Rosie Flores
1988	"Somebody Loses, Somebody Wins"	67	
	"He Cares"	74	single only

Source http://en.wikipedia.org/wiki/Rosie_Flores

Scotty Moore

Birth name	Winfield Scott Moore III
Born	December 27, 1931 Gadsden, Tennessee, USA
Genres	Rock and roll
Occupations	Guitarist
Years active	1950s–2007
Labels	Sun
Associated acts	Elvis Presley The Blue Moon Boys, Ricky Nelson, Ten Years After
Website	Scotty Moore website

Winfield Scott "Scotty" Moore III (born December 27, 1931) is an American guitarist. He is best known for his backing of Elvis Presley in the first part of his career, between 1954 and the beginning of Elvis' Hollywood years. He was ranked 44th in *Rolling Stone* magazine's list of 100 Greatest Guitarists of All Time in 2011. He was inducted into the Rock And Roll Hall of Fame (category: sideman) in 2000.

Career

Scotty Moore was born near Gadsden, Tennessee. He learned to play the guitar from family and friends at eight years of age. Although underage when he enlisted, Moore served in the United States Navy between 1948 and 1952.

Moore's early background was in jazz and country music. A fan of guitarist Chet Atkins, Moore led a group called the "Starlite Wranglers" before Sam Phillips at Sun Records put him together with then teenage Elvis Presley. Phillips believed that Moore's lead guitar and Bill Black's double bass were all that was needed to augment Presley's rhythm guitar and lead vocals on their recordings. In 1954 Moore and Black accompanied Elvis on what would become the first legendary Presley hit, the Sun Studios session cut of "That's All Right (Mama)", a recording regarded as a seminal event in rock and roll history. Elvis, Black and Moore then formed the Blue Moon Boys.

For a time, Moore served as Elvis's personal manager. They were later joined by drummer D.J. Fontana. Beginning in July 1954, the Blue Moon Boys toured and recorded throughout the American South and, as Presley's popularity rose, they toured the United States and made appearances in various Presley television shows and motion pictures. The Blue Moon Boys, including Moore, appear in the few 1955 home movie clips that survive of Elvis before he achieved national recognition. Moore, Black, and Fontana also appear on the Dorsey Brothers, Milton Berle, Steve Allen, and Ed Sullivan live TV shows of January 1956 to January 1957, and also reunite on the 1960 Timex TV special with Frank Sinatra welcoming Elvis' return from the Army.

Moore played on many of Presley's most famous recordings, including "Good Rockin' Tonight", "Baby Let's Play House", "Heartbreak Hotel", "Mystery Train", "Hound Dog", "Too Much" and "Jailhouse Rock". Moore and the Blue Moon Boys also perform (and have additional small walk-in and speaking roles) with Elvis in three of his movies (*Loving You*, *Jailhouse Rock*, and *King Creole*) filmed in 1957 and 1958.

In 1964, Moore released a solo album on Epic Records called *The Guitar That Changed the World*, played using his Gibson Super 400. He performed on the NBC television special known as the '68 Comeback Special, again with his Gibson Super 400 which was also played by Elvis.

For his pioneering contribution, Moore has been recognized by the Rockabilly Hall of Fame. In 2000, he was inducted into the Rock and Roll Hall of Fame.

Style and influence

Moore's playing on his Gibson with his unique finger-picking style with pick at same time, as on the Sun and early RCA recordings, was unique and exciting, representing a move of the Chet Atkins style into a more rockabilly mode. Moore's best performances are often considered precedent-setting.

Moore is given credit as the pioneer of the rock 'n' roll lead guitarist. Many popular guitarists cite Moore as the performer that brought the lead guitarist to a dominant role in a rock 'n' roll band. Although some lead guitarists/vocalists, such as Chuck Berry and blues legend BB King, had gained popularity by the 1950s, Presley rarely played his own lead while performing, instead providing rhythm guitar and leaving the lead duties to Moore. As a guitarist, Moore was a noticeable presence in Presley's performances, despite his introverted demeanor. He became an inspiration to many subsequent popular guitarists, including Bruce Springsteen and Keith Richards of the Rolling Stones. While Moore was working on his memoir with co-author James L. Dickerson, Richards told Dickerson, "Everyone else wanted to be Elvis--I wanted to be Scotty." Richards has stated many times (*Rolling Stone* magazine, *Life* autobiography) that he could never figure out how to play the "stop time" break and figure that Moore plays on "I'm Left, You're Right, She's Gone" (Sun), and that he hopes it will remain a mystery.

Equipment

While with Presley, Moore initially played a Gibson ES-295 (nicknamed "The Guitar that Changed the World"), before switching to a Gibson L5 and subsequently a Gibson Super 400.

One of the key pieces of equipment in Moore's sound on many of the recordings with Elvis, besides his guitars, was the use of the Ray Butts EchoSonic, a guitar amplifier with a tape echo built in, which allowed him to take his trademark slapback echo on the road.

Portrayal in popular culture

Mark Adam portrayed Moore in the 2005 CBS miniseries *Elvis*.

Emory Smith portrayed Moore in the 1981 documentary film *This is Elvis*.

Jesse Dabson played Scotty Moore in the 1990 ABC television series *Elvis: The Early Years*.

The book *That's Alright, Elvis: The Untold Story of Elvis's First Guitarist and Manager*, is written by Scotty Moore as told to James Dickerson. A recent book called *The Blue Moon Boys* also tells the story of Moore, Black, and Fontana before, during and after their tenure with Elvis.

Compositions

Scotty Moore co-wrote the songs "My Kind of Carrying On" and "Now She Cares No More" which were released as Sun 202 on Sun Records in 1954 when he was a member of the group Doug Poindexter and the Starlite Wranglers with Bill Black as the bassist. He co-wrote the instrumental "Have Guitar Will Travel" in 1958 with Bill Black, which was released as a 45 single 107, on the Fernwood Records label.

Source http://en.wikipedia.org/wiki/Scotty_Moore

Sonny Fisher

Therman "Sonny" Fisher (November 13, 1931, Chandler, Texas – October 8, 2005, Houston, Texas) was an American singer, songwriter, and guitarist.

He was inducted into the Rockabilly Hall of Fame.

Fun facts: He was actually born in 1930, but his mother didn't record his birth until a year after. He has 7 children, and raised one of his grandchildren, Danny Fisher. He sold his home on the San Jacinto river after tropical depression Allison destroyed it.

Source http://en.wikipedia.org/wiki/Sonny_Fisher

Tommy Allsup

Tommy Allsup

Allsup in 2009
Background information
Born   November 24, 1931

	Owasso, Oklahoma, US
Genres	Rock and roll, country, Country-Rock
Occupations	Musician, producer
Instruments	Guitar
Years active	1949–present
Labels	Liberty
Associated acts	Buddy Holly, Waylon Jennings

Tommy Allsup (born November 24, 1931 in Owasso, Oklahoma) is an American musician.

He worked with entertainers such as Buddy Holly and Bob Wills & His Texas Playboys. He moved to Los Angeles, played with local bands, and did session work, including writing credit for the Ventures', "Guitar Twist'.

He returned to Odessa, Texas, where he worked with Ronnie Smith, and Roy Orbison, and producing Willie Nelson. In 1958, he moved to Nashville, where he did session work, and produced Bob Wills', "24 Great Hits by Bob Wills and His Texas Playboys". In 1979, he started a club, "Tommy's Heads Up Saloon", in Fort Worth. The club was named after a coin flip Allsup had with Ritchie Valens on February 2, 1959 that saved Allsup's life.

Source http://en.wikipedia.org/wiki/Tommy_Allsup